CULTURE BATTLES

CULTURE BATTLES

Victim or Victor, Your Choice

PAUL H. WEAVER

Birmingham, Alabama

Culture Battles

Brookstone Publishing Group
An imprint of Iron Stream Media
100 Missionary Ridge
Birmingham, AL 35242
IronStreamMedia.com

Library of Congress Control Number: 2023914686

Cover design by twolineSTUDIO.com

ISBN: 978-1-960814-02-9 (paperback)
ISBN: 978-1-960814-03-6 (ebook)

1 2 3 4 5—28 27 26 25 24 23

Dedication

This book is dedicated to the great people who chose to work with me over the past 40 years. Their buy-in to our culture and core values has made possible the 50-year success journey at Weaver Leather.

Thank You

To my wife, Gladys, and my editor, Elaine Starner, for taking my handwritten copy and making something that will be valued and look professional. Thanks to Gladys for the much-needed encouragement and last, but certainly not least, for her proofreading skills, which are quite incredible. Great job, ladies. I couldn't have done this without you.

CONTENTS

INTRODUCTION

In every entity, be it family, church, business, community, or country, there must be what I would call culture warriors, those who preserve and demonstrate the core values which they hold dear.

Our country is as divided as it has ever been since the Civil War in 1861. Our forefathers named us the United States of America. That term is no longer a snapshot of this great nation. Today we are the Divided States of America. So how did this happen over the past 150 years?

What started out as a country formed on Judeo-Christian values has slowly eroded over these years, and today our leaders proudly proclaim that we are no longer a Christian nation and we are now a secular country, free from the bondage of Christianity. When presidential candidates confidently say that America's best days are still ahead of us, do not believe it.

How could this happen to the strongest democracy in the world? Edmund Burke said it so well when he said, "The only thing necessary for evil to triumph in the world is that good men do nothing." The "good men" he was talking about are the average, hard-working Americans whose core values are derived from God's Word, the Bible. And if we speak out against evil, we become prey for those promoting evil.

But we have influence in our homes, our communities, and our businesses, and we are the culture warriors who can bring about change on a local level that becomes a lighthouse for people searching for a better way. We may be vastly outnumbered, but when did Almighty God ever need great numbers to accomplish His work? Never. He always chose a small number of dedicated men and women to carry out His mission.

This book is a challenge to be bold and courageous and never be intimidated in speaking the truth.

We are in a war against evil, and we may lose some or many of the battles. But we win the war. Guaranteed! In the end, God Himself will rule the world with justice. In the meantime, we are to create the good culture that becomes the salt and light of this world.

CULTURE BATTLES

The family is both the fundamental unit of society as well as the root of culture.

—Marianne E. Neifert

Chapter 1

The Family: Birthplace of Culture

When I was an eight-year-old kid, my best friend lived just up the road from our family, and I biked up to their place on many occasions. They were farmers and didn't have their breakfast till after the milking was done, so at times I would make a presence before the morning meal was over. They were probably annoyed that I would be there so early, but they were always gracious and kind to me. The conversation among the kids and parents was pleasant and very interesting for me to observe. After breakfast, the father would read a little Scripture and then pray for the family and for the day ahead.

That was my first look at a really good culture in a home. As a matter of fact, I thought it was too good to be true and that they were surely putting on a good front because I was there. But if this was actually for real, I decided there and then that I would want to have that in my home someday.

When our lives begin, our culture starts shaping us from day one. Children born into a good home with two loving parents have a good start at forming a solid foundation of security and trust that produces wellness and happiness. As these children grow and mature, they become a product of their environment and the culture of their home. That is the norm, but there are exceptions to this that can be attributed to genetics and the friends that they hang out with as kids and teenagers. For this reason, the family culture in these formative years is so very important to our kids.

My friend and his siblings grew up, and they all married good partners. Three of the boys ended up being pastors as their dad was. Even at this early age, the picture of a great family culture made a serious impact on me and I was saddened by the fact that our home was not at all like that.

In my case, the home I was born into was tumultuous and not a happy home. Dad and Mom were usually not in agreement on the parenting side of things. Dad was quick tempered, and his response to most infractions against his law and order was severe punishments such as beatings and verbal abuse. The word *love* was never spoken, and he was rarely in a good frame of mind. This set the stage for a toxic culture we experienced as children and young adults. Church and religion also played a big part in our growing up. Needless to say, my views of both church and religion were less than enthusiastic due to my vow to never follow in my dad's footsteps in regards to parenting. All of my siblings as well have suffered from the culture of the home we grew up in.

At the age of 19, I married a young lady who came from a home with a great culture. The difference between our families was like night and day, and both homes affected the futures of their children in some very significant ways that have reached into following generations. The siblings of my wife's family all loved each other, and even now, in their seventies, they still do. Their relationships with each other are a testament to their home life during their formative years. Their parents were not perfect, but they were far above the norm in loving their children. The parents' love for each other was really the starting point for the outstanding culture in their home. When the last and youngest daughter got married, their dad composed a poem that was titled, "It's Hard to See the Last One Go." He recited this poem at the reception, and by the time he came to the end, he was in tears. The family sang and played music together, and the siblings grew up as a cohesive unit. After my wife's mom and dad passed away, the tradition was not broken. Every week they continue to get together, have a coffee break, visit, work on their 1000-piece puzzles, and just have fun spending time with one another.

These stark differences demonstrate that culture rules in the family. Culture is formed by our own core values, and our core values have been formed, many times, by the culture we grew up in. This generational cycle underscores the importance of breaking the negative patterns of a bad home life that influence children in those crucial early years. **For most of us, the die is cast as to how we see life and react to situations by the time we are ten years old.** As we mature and gain knowledge and wisdom, we will surely see the world through different eyes. However, our childhood still plays a vital role in how we respond to life's challenges.

Think for a moment about what happened in your first ten years of life that still influences you as an adult. That influence has been for both the good and the bad. My dad was a giver and enjoyed helping people. I watched him do that, and it deeply influenced what I do today. On the downside, he was impatient, and his intolerance made him quick on the trigger in dealing with people. Guess what? I'm the same way. He saw things in black and white with little to no gray area in his beliefs. I do that as well.

The fact is that no parent is perfect, and no matter how hard we try, we sometimes do things that bring negative elements into the culture of our home that will affect our children down the road. This is all the more reason for us to maintain a course of continuous improvement. When we need to make positive changes in ourselves, it is better to simply do so and let our life speak than to try to teach what we ourselves have not mastered. Our children are much more perceptive than we think they are. The saying "More is caught than taught" is very true.

So the question is, what are your core values? In other words, what principles dominate your life? Face it, life is a series of chain reactions. Our core values establish our motives, our motives establish our actions, and our actions shape the culture we develop in our homes, work, church, and society. If you want to do an evaluation of who you really are and develop an accurate self-awareness, go to the appendix in this book and read about the 48 character principles that can reset your life and change your core values and the culture that you bring to the table.

> There is no doubt that it is around the family and the home that all the greatest virtues, the most dominating virtues of humans, are created, strengthened and maintained.
> —Winston Churchill

ꕤ

Strong marriages are good for everyone: they not only benefit the individuals who are part of these relationships but also will strengthen their whole society. Throughout history, marriage has been the foundational building block of every society and culture. **When marriages have been strong, nations have been strong. When marriages and families weaken, cultures decline.**

God also uses marriage to strengthen character. In successful relationships, we learn to be unselfish and loving. For those who get married, there is no other human relationship that will have a greater impact on their lives. The Bible says in Romans 12:9-10, "Don't just pretend to love others. Really love them. Hate what is wrong. Hold tightly to what is good. Love each other with genuine affection, and take delight in honoring each other." Does this sound like the average family and marriage of today?

What we are seeing in our world today is the opposite of that nourishing culture. The world we live in is way off track. The national culture now being established is toxic and will likely be the demise of our great country—and it all starts in ourselves and our homes.

Children are born into single-parent homes where fathers are often missing in action. The lack of mother and father united in parenting with great core values is at the very root of our problems. The bad culture in homes can stem from one or multiple generations past, and it keeps getting passed on to each new generation. To break the cycle, someone—be it the husband or the wife—will need to come to the realization that their past is dictating not only their future but the future of their children. If the father, who should be the spiritual and cultural leader of the home, decides to stop this deadly cycle and turn to his heavenly Father for help and guidance, then and then only can the culture of the home improve.

Many times when one person makes the effort to turn his life around, the positive change will influence the rest of the family to sit up and take notice of the improved culture, and other family members may then decide to follow that person's lead. Absence of good leadership based upon the absolute truths found only in the Bible will lead to generations of family cultures based on bad character.

There are many stories of abused children who have no roadmap for finding success in their lives and their futures. These drifting and directionless children are headed for some pretty tough times as they grow up and seek a culture that will accept them. Gangs and a life of crime can take root, and kids end up in our prison systems after engaging in illegal activities or dealing drugs. Night after night, the evening news has stories and videos of violent crimes committed by young teenagers. Carjackings, murders, and countless other crimes by lawless kids headed for a life of crime and imprisonment. They have hard eyes that look like the eyes of seasoned criminals, and their lives are meaningless. They would rather steal than work.

Often fathers are to blame for not raising and guiding the children they have sired. They simply abandon them and move on to the next woman to impregnate. Even animals are more responsible than many fathers. When an adult male elephant abandons its offspring, the young elephants turn unruly and violent. At some point, an older adult male will step in and act as a father to these young elephants. They will punish them for bad behavior and teach them how to interact with others. The young elephants respond to this eagerly and change their ways. If an elephant can get it right, it makes you wonder why mankind is so often guilty of neglecting the care of their offspring. Not all of these scenarios arise from bad homes, but the majority do.

Our government also carries blame in many of these circumstances. To pay someone to live if they are a single mom but not if they are married is just one of the many ways our lawmakers have steered us to where we are today. We will always reap a crop of the seeds that were sown. To sow seeds that caused our innocent children to live in a bad culture will produce more children who share the same fate. The government has never been the savior of the poor and underprivileged.

The church, on the other hand, was formed thousands of years ago to bring the body of believers together to teach the Word, to enjoy fellowship with like-minded Christ followers, and to grow into an important community place to worship. The church was and is often called a family because its people are tightly knit, looking out for each other, praying for each other, visiting the sick, helping parents provide homes with a good culture, and setting the young people up for success in life. The church has played a vital role in the development of our country and for our families and communities. Today we not only have local churches, we also have access to many great Christian pastors we can tune into online. But we cannot ignore the importance of being involved in a church body where people are there to help and encourage us and to attend regularly with our families. Without this, our culture as families and on a greater scale, our nation's culture will suffer greatly. We were never meant to be lone rangers, and we will never reach our full potential without being affiliated with a Bible-teaching church that gives us a solid foundation.

One of the reasons the church was established was to change lives and set those lives on the path toward a victorious future. Through the church's teachings and the people who belong to this body of believers, we fulfill our calling to be the light in a dark world, a place where individuals can come and experience fellowship and provide good counsel for those who are going down the wrong road. It is there for those who need help, spiritual guidance, friendship, discipleship, and support, even counseling or monetary help. That was the plan set in motion 2,000 years ago. And today, that plan is the antidote that creates good culture and makes the world a better place.

Not only do we have the church community as a help to our families, we also have countless Christian teachers online who provide a wealth of information regarding family dynamics. But we must care enough to make it a priority to become a culture-rich family.

Our church had a series on parenting some years ago, and I was saddened by the fact that I was hearing this after our kids were grown up and had left home. What a difference it would have made. I especially enjoyed the little article written by Andy Stanley on the four stages of parenting. (The four stages are his; the comments are mine.)

For years 1-5: Discipline. Children do not come equipped with great character. They learn very well on their own to throw fits of rage when they don't get what they want. (Go to Walmart and see this in real life.) They learn very quickly to lie and grab things away from other kids. They pick up on bad language the parents or other kids use, and they use their profanity vocabulary proudly. Bottom line, discipline is not a popular word in our society, and it shows. The model today is for kids to "find their way." Well, they will find a way, but it won't be the right way. Between birth and five years old, the child will either know about the God we serve or will be confused about the real origins of life and will find it hard to be disciplined in anything they do.

For years 5-12: Training. The Bible says, "Train up a child in the way he should go; and when he is old, he will not depart from it" (Proverbs 22:6 KJV). But don't expect your kids to do as you teach them, if you yourself don't do what you teach. Case in point: One of our senior leaders in the company came to work one day and told me his young son had blurted out a bit of profanity that shocked him. He told his son not to say that again and asked where he had heard the word. To his surprise, the little guy said, "I heard it from you." In disbelief, his father asked the boy when he heard him say it. The young son said, "Oh, Dad, you say it all the time when you're on the lawnmower!" Needless to say, Dad thought the noise of the mower would drown out the words he uttered when he ran over something or he and the machine weren't seeing eye to eye. The occasional chunk of gravel in the lawn was really detrimental to the freshly sharpened blades, and his comments then were heard and repeated by his attentive son. (By the way, that dad could have been me.)

For years 12-18: Coaching. This stage of life is so very important for our children. It is a difficult age for them as they go from happy-go-lucky kids totally dependent upon mom and dad for all their needs to teenagers going through the changes of becoming an adult both in mind and body. For me this was a difficult time. I was strong willed, did not have a sense of being loved by my dad, and was torn between wanting to do what was right and not wanting to do what Dad thought was right. Remember, our home had a culture of toxic anger over non-important issues, and I was counting the days when I could move out of our home and experience some freedom from my repressive childhood. In addition, I was confused by the teachings of our church, which preached the truth but added lots of man-made junk. Forced to look and dress in ways that the church dictated, I was made a target in school. I was made fun of for looking like a geek while other kids looked and dressed in what was the norm those days. This made me angry and resentful of my dad, and I went out of my way to make him as miserable as I was. He was in a real conundrum, secretly liking the fact that I was no pushover, but knowing that I made him look bad in the eyes of his church people. His simple refusal to allow me a say in who I was or how I looked was unacceptable to me. Little did I know that there was actually Scripture to back me up. In Ephesians chapter 6 verse 4, the Amplified Bible instructs:

> Fathers, do not provoke your children to anger. [Do not exasperate them to the point of resentment with demands that are trivial or unreasonable or humiliating or abusive; nor by showing favoritism or indifference to any of them], but bring them up [tenderly, with loving kindness] in the discipline and instruction of the Lord.

Coaching is being supportive, sharing life experiences, and teaching the truth. Believe in the person you're coaching, be their cheerleader when they win, and comfort them in their losses. Young people in this age group are very intuitive; they know if you really love them for who they are or if your love for them is conditional based on their performance. In this period of a young person's life, making mistakes is to be expected. Help them sort out what went wrong, and be there to lend a helping hand. That's coaching. They will cherish this time of their life now and in the future and will perpetuate this culture with their own children. It's really simple. Teaching them to be great parents by being a great parent is the highest form of coaching. If our actions don't match what we teach, we're hypocrites. The good coach can often influence his children without saying a word.

At 18+ years: Friendship. As our children go into adulthood, a good, solid relationship based on friendship with our sons and daughters provides stability and a real sense of wellness for parents, children, and grandchildren. Nowhere is the good-culture principle more evident than when a family stays close and connected when the children are now adults with their own families.

It's good to remember that even when they are grown, they will always be your children, and your parental instinct will still want to protect them from bad things. But, much as we would like to save them from headaches and heartaches, they are now on their own, and advice should be given sparingly and by request. If there was a good relationship while they were living at home, they will probably ask for advice. If there wasn't a good relationship at home, you can forget about advice-giving. Counsel will not be asked for or accepted when offered. Our kids have both been married for twenty years or more, and Gladys and I love them, their spouses, and our grandkids dearly and want the very best for them. But their choices in life are their own, and if they stumble and fall—well, so did we. Neither my parents nor Gladys's parents meddled in our family affairs or in our careers. For that I am grateful.

I can honestly say that I have good memories of our kids growing up and then going through the stages of becoming adults and parents. I hope the culture in our home has been a help to them. We as parents were not perfect by any means, but they never had to guess if we loved each other and respected each other as man and wife and as parents. I love this quote by Kathleen Billings: "The greatest gift we can give our children is to love our spouse." A strong marriage, where love between a husband and wife is not only visible but felt in the home, gives our children security and stability. Chances are, they will pass that culture on to their families as well.

Even though my experience of home as a child and teenager did not follow this guide for a happy family, my relationship with Dad ended well and all is forgiven. Dad believed in me and helped me grow the little business that he had started. Without him, there would be no Weaver Leather. Mom loved me and was the safe place to fall when things went bad for me. They both loved the Lord, and I plan to see them on the other side.

The glory of the gospel is that when the church is absolutely different from the world, she invariably attracts it.

—Martyn Lloyd-Jones

Chapter 2

The Church and Its Purpose

As my wife and I ride around rural America on our motorcycle, we see many small old church buildings. Most of them are no longer in use and have been replaced by fewer but much larger complexes that serve bigger geographical areas. That's understandable, given our better and faster means of transportation than what was available hundreds of years ago. The world we live in has changed, and sadly the culture has also changed drastically.

Over the past 246 years, the church has played a vital role in our country. Much of the positive in our culture as a country was due to a vibrant church. The church provided the teachings of the Bible, giving our country a moral compass. It helped people in need, cared for the sick and elderly, and was the platform of evangelism.

The government is now responsible for many of our needs such as unemployment, disability, health insurance, education, and a list that goes on and on. Half of our income is paid out in taxes for those services, and now, beyond all this, the arm of the government is dictating what we can and cannot do or say.

When churches talk about sin (and fewer and fewer do talk about it), our culture wants to "cancel" us, or shut us down. Standing up to the evil that is so prevalent today is not popular. Churches are no longer the great reformers, but are now conformers. Messages now are self-help messages, with specific Bible verses used only to drive home a point.

Recently our campus pastor, Dan Wigton, delivered a powerful message that took us back to a time when the church used the Bible as the text. It illustrated the sharp contrast between where the church began and where it is today. The Scripture for the basis of the message was found in the book of Daniel in the Old Testament, the story of three young Hebrew men whose nation had been overthrown by a heathen king.

In 605 BC, King Nebuchadnezzar of Babylon captured Jerusalem and brought back the best and brightest of his conquests. Enter Shadrach, Meshach, and Abednego. In Babylon, these three young Hebrew men were trained, coached, and elevated to top positions in the administration. These guys were then wealthy, powerful, and prosperous. Life was good. Whenever you get comfortable, Christ followers, be ready: the fire is coming.

King Nebuchadnezzar went on a major ego trip and had a statue made of himself, 90 feet high and 9 feet wide, in solid gold. He planned a dedication ceremony in which the band's first tune was the cue for everyone in Babylon to bow down and worship the king's statue. The penalty for not bowing down was to be thrown into a blazing furnace and burned alive.

So the music played, and though the king's mandate said that everyone of all nations and languages must bow down, Shadrach, Meshach, and Abednego stood tall. They worshipped the true God, the God they knew from their homeland, and they did not bow.

Here I'd like to point out that **the opposite of conviction is always compromise.** Compromise is always easier. It feels natural to want to do what everyone else is doing. It's what feels "right," and so you pretend to believe something you don't really believe because it is the popular thing to do. That's compromise. Conviction is usually difficult, lonely, and doesn't feel "right."

So the three young Hebrew men stood for what was right, did not compromise, and did not bow down. And what happened? The Cancel Culture Crowd was up in arms.

> "But there are some Jews—Shadrach, Meshach and Abednego—whom you have put in charge of the province of Babylon. They pay no attention to you, Your Majesty. They refuse to serve your gods and do not worship the gold statue you have set up." (Daniel 3:12)

Those three Jewish men were leaders in Babylon, but they had critics and they had enemies. They had refused to adopt the culture and religious practices of Babylon, and they stood out. Today, we might say their critics wanted to cancel them. Bottom line: In today's culture, we will always have enemies when we stand for what is right. We become targets, and the pressure to cave in becomes intense.

How do you respond when the pressure of this world begins to circle you like a tiger shark? Or, as in the case of these three young men, when the fire is stoked hotter and hotter?

> Then Nebuchadnezzar flew into a rage and ordered that Shadrach, Meshach, and Abednego be brought before him. When they were brought in, Nebuchadnezzar said to them, "Is it true, Shadrach, Meshach, and Abednego that you refuse to serve my gods or to worship the gold statue I have set up? I will give you one more chance to bow down and worship the statue I have made when you hear the sound of the musical instruments. But if you refuse, you will be thrown immediately into the blazing furnace. And then what god will be able to rescue you from my power?" (Daniel 3:13-15)

What is our reaction and response when we are faced with critics who are angry and envious of our confidence?

My second point is that **true convictions lead to unshakeable confidence.**

Check out the confidence Shadrach, Meschach, and Abednego had in their convictions. They weren't worried. They had decided early on what they were going to do. Their convictions and confidence were stronger than the king's, and it made him nervous enough to give them a second chance. He asked the million-dollar question, which is really another way of saying, "Which do you fear more, God's hand or mine?"

So let's hit the pause button for a second. Let's move the story to America in 2022. Who or what do you fear? God, or the opinions of this world? The truths of Scripture, or the trends of social media? Many Christians and churches would bow down quickly. "We don't want to cause division. We won't really be worshiping Nebuchadnezzar if we bow. I mean, how can we ever reach people if we take a stand and make them mad at us? Look, everyone online is liking and sharing this image of the 90-foot gold statue. Look at the ratio for Nebuchadnezzar! We need to keep the peace and unity." There will always be excuses, and you can always create justification to get in line with the popular point of view.

> Shadrach, Meshach, and Abednego replied, "O Nebuchadnezzar, we do not need to defend ourselves before you. If we are thrown into the blazing furnace, the God whom we serve is able to save us. He will rescue us from your power, Your Majesty. But even if he doesn't, we want to make it clear to you, Your Majesty, that we will never serve your gods or worship the gold statue you have set up." (Daniel 3:16-17)

Now, these guys have faith. We all claim to have faith in God. But the devil wants us to have a fragile faith, a faith that fails when the heat rises, a cautious faith that wakes up each day and puts God on trial, saying, "Okay, we'll see how you act today and if you get to be my God."

Don't miss this part of the story: The three young men knew King Nebuchadnezzar would respond, but they did not know what God would do. They feared God more than men. They respected the king, but they trusted and believed in God. They were more concerned about being biblically correct than politically correct. They were ready to say goodbye to the king and Babylon.

Here is the question: Who do you respect? Who do you fear? Just as in Babylon, our world demands allegiance. You can't straddle the fence. We live in a day and age of "tolerance." But tolerance in our society doesn't mean just agreeing to disagree or respecting a different opinion. No, the world demands that you accept immoral lifestyles, you must celebrate sin. God's Word, for example, says marriage is between a man and a woman, and sex is to be inside of that marriage. Our Babylonian US culture says, "No, no, no! We will redefine marriage, we will celebrate all things sexual outside of marriage. You must accept, you will approve, you will bow down when the music plays—or face the fire."

These three guys stared political correctness right in the face, and we can do the same in our churches. The church should preach love and the forgiveness of Jesus to everyone. His forgiveness covers whatever you've done. As His followers, we treat everyone with love and respect. But we must draw a line in the sand. We don't want people to walk away without knowing the truth. We can love a person and still not approve of a sinful lifestyle. The church has to have that confidence in truth in this difficult time.

Where does your tolerance end? Shadrach, Meshach, and Abednego tolerated a name change; these were Babylonian names given to them, not their birth names. They tolerated living in a different culture and country and under a pagan king; they tolerated the training and even being a part of Nebuchadnezzar's government. But when it came down to worshiping a false god of this world, they said no. They drew a line in the sand. When was the last time you drew a line in the sand against the popular thinking of today because you knew what the Bible said and you were not going to compromise?

> Nebuchadnezzar was so furious with Shadrach, Meshach, and Abednego that his face became distorted with rage. He commanded that the furnace be heated seven times hotter than usual. Then he ordered some of the strongest men of his army to bind Shadrach, Meshach, and Abednego and throw them into the blazing furnace. So they tied them up and threw them into the furnace, fully dressed in their pants, turbans, robes, and other garments. And because the king, in his anger had demanded such a hot fire in the furnace, the flames killed the soldiers as they threw the three men in. So Shadrach, Meshach, and Abednego, securely tied, fell into the roaring flames.
>
> But suddenly, Nebuchadnezzar jumped up in amazement and exclaimed to his advisers, "Didn't we tie up three men and throw them into the furnace?"
>
> "Yes, Your Majesty, we certainly did," they replied.
>
> "Look!" Nebuchadnezzar shouted. "I see four men, unbound, walking around in the fire unharmed! And the fourth looks like a god!"
>
> Then Nebuchadnezzar came as close as he could to the door of the flaming furnace and shouted: "Shadrach, Meshach, and Abednego, servants of the Most High God, come out! Come here!"
>
> So Shadrach, Meshach, and Abednego stepped out of the fire. Then the high officers, officials, governors, and advisers crowded around them and saw that the fire had not touched

> them. Not a hair on their heads was singed, and their clothing was not scorched. They didn't even smell of smoke!
>
> Then Nebuchadnezzar said, "Praise to the God of Shadrach, Meshach, and Abednego! He sent his angel to rescue his servants who trusted in him. They defied the king's command and were willing to die rather than serve or worship any god except their own God. Therefore, I make this decree: If any people, whatever their race or nation or language, speak a word against the God of Shadrach, Meshach, and Abednego, they will be torn limb from limb, and their houses will be turned into heaps of rubble. There is no other god who can rescue like this!"
>
> Then the king promoted Shadrach, Meshach, and Abednego to even higher positions in the province of Babylon. (Daniel 3:19-30)

When strength in the name of Almighty God prevails, nothing can keep His church from prospering and growing. Instead of playing defense, we should be playing offense. After all, we know the outcome of this battle that rages on. We win! Not only do we win, we get to rule and reign over all the earth with God himself for 1,000 years. So if I had one word to describe the church as it was intended to be, it would be *fearless.*

Yet, instead of facing the reality that we, the church, are under attack from all sides, the church for the most part is silent and totally avoids even talking about the evil we face daily.

We are privileged to live in this unprecedented time in history. Events prophesied in the Bible are coming to pass in a way they never have before. The signs and wonders are all around us. For the church to be silent in this age is nothing short of cowardice. There are churches who are teaching the truth in its fullness, but they are not the majority. Strength, boldness, courage, and absolute truths are magnets that draw to any strong movement.

May this become the church's culture in this season. If history repeats itself (as it always has), the culture of the church is always strengthened in times of hardship and persecution.

We should be proactive and reform the modern-day church as a whole and decide now that we will never bend or bow to the world's demands. The greatest enemy of courage and faith is an easy life with no testing of what we believe. This creates apathy. But most courageous decisions are made in advance, so when the time comes for us to make these critical decisions, we will already know exactly what we must do.

As a rule, the policy of most megachurches is to stay away from politics. They do not talk about our world situation and what is happening in our own republic. We are living in unprecedented times and our country is in complete disarray. To not warn our people of the peril that we face and will be subject to is simply unthinkable. I am not talking about what most people will label as politics; I am talking about the evil that is invading our nation.

The millions of abortions being performed in our country is not a political issue, it is a sin. When God wrote the Ten Commandments with His finger on stone tablets, the commands were simple, and they are still in place. "Thou shalt not kill." That's not political, that is God's law. Tens of millions of dead babies is genocide. This shows the extent to which the leadership in our country is willing to go in furthering the cause of the evil one. On January 11, 2023, the House passed a bill that would require that all infants born alive after attempted abortions get medical care. The measure, titled "The Born-Alive Abortion Survivors Protection Act," passed by a vote of 220 to 210 to 1. Not a single Democrat voted to support the bill. The only representative who did not vote against the bill voted "present." This is the razor-thin margin that exists between life and death of the innocent.

I fully believe we are entering a time of sin and chaos on a scale that neither we nor our forefathers have seen or imagined. In our culture, evil is called good and good is called evil. Our kids and grandkids are bombarded with teaching that is meant to deceive and destroy. As God's church, we should be warning and teaching people the disturbing truth that the fires of unrest are actually being fueled by the turmoil we see on our streets and the leadership we now have in place. "For we are not fighting against flesh-and-blood enemies, but against evil rulers and authorities of the unseen world, against mighty powers in this dark world, and against evil spirits in the heavenly places." (Ephesians 6:12).

So what is the function of the church in terms of being a culture compass for the communities they serve? Now, this list does not come from a website or from any pastor or church-growth seminar. It comes from being 70 years old and from a lay person's point of view. I have been in many different types of denominational churches that follow an agreed-upon standard on how churches that fall under the same umbrella will operate and how they are to teach their congregations. We now attend a non-denominational church with multiple off-site campuses. So my perspective on the church's mission may differ from that of a pastor.

The church must teach and preach the Gospel *in its entirety* if it hopes to fulfill its mission:

1) **To instill, develop, and grow core values that will guide people through life.** These values will help to establish a healthy culture in homes and in so doing will create homes that are a beacon of light their neighbors and friends can learn and benefit from. These core values will strengthen marriages and family ties and create a barrier against the evil one. A loving father

and mother will teach their children how to live a bountiful life. The family becomes a closely-knit, caring family unit that will go on for generations to come.

If the enemy can bring chaos and division into the home, then he will cause marriages to fail and kids to live in uncertainty. For evil to flourish, it seeks to divide and conquer. Families who attend church together regularly will have a much better chance that the kids will follow the same pattern when they leave home and start their own families. When Dad and Mom are actively involved in the church, the chances of the kids following that example are high. If only the dad attends church, the percentage of children continuing to attend drops, and if both of the parents neglect this important part of their lives, the chances of children staying in church go down to a very small percentage. Our examples show how important faith and Christianity are in our lives, and when our families can see us living out that faith, they are much more likely to buy into those values and continue them into the next generation.

2) **To be the search engine to bring non-believers to faith and to grow them to bring others in with them.** This describes an *evangelical* church. It is a church that grows, not because of fancy buildings or entertainment-type music, but because it has established a culture of wanting to help people in sickness or hard times, through caring service and the prayers we provide as a part of the body of Christ. The most receptive people to minister to are those who need help physically, have lost a love one, have fallen on hard times financially, or have had something traumatic happen in their lives. Hurting people are seeking help—and that's where the church shines.

Our Amish community does this to perfection. When a storm or fire destroys a house or barns or when someone is injured, the Amish are there helping, feeding, cleaning up, or giving shelter to victims. Buildings are repaired or rebuilt with many people donating time, money, and resources. They even have their own health care, funded through members' tithes and giving. Unlike insurance companies that make money on our premiums and the health care providers, this service runs on zero dollars of profit and gets them the lowest health care rates available because none of it pads an insurance company's pockets. Their community care for each other is one big reason they have such a high rate of retention among their young people.

3) **To warn us about the penalties of sin.** Evil is causing havoc in the world and every part of our country. And this is where I take issue on where the church stands today. I don't want to paint this with a broad brush and include all churches because there are churches that do speak out against sin and evil. However, I would guess the majority are consciously avoiding these issues because it may be offensive to some. Growth, attendance, and financial support drive these concerns. I read a quote many years ago that speaks to this very plainly: "There was a time when people went to church, heard the truth, and wept over their sins. Today, people go to church, hear a motivational speech, and ignore their sins" (source unknown). This is the weakest link in the church's mission today, the place where they are completely missing the target in their responsibility.

I call it "failure to warn," as trial lawyers would say. No one can stop someone from living in sin; not even God will stop them because He gives us a choice. But the Bible is full of warnings and is very specific about right and wrong. To only teach the "do" parts of the Bible and omit the "don'ts" is not only not biblical, it is the omission of a very important part of our lives. God Himself wrote the Ten Commandments on stone with His finger. Look them up in your Bible. They are found in Exodus 20:3-17 and Deuteronomy 5:6-21. Our culture today, including some churches, chooses to ignore these because they are found in the Old Testament and are not believed to be relevant in today's modern society. The shameful thing is that some churches and well-known pastors have bought into that myth. I can fully understand why society has ditched these as archaic and no longer true and applicable; if so, society can redefine truth as whatever they say it is and not what the Bible teaches. I can understand that the mind of a carnal person believes this because these promptings and beliefs are not of God but of the evil one himself, the father of all lies and deception. However, for the church to appease and not confront this deception head on is, in my opinion, nothing short of heresy. And those churches will surely be held accountable.

Pressure from the media and our lawmakers should have no effect on us; we are to speak God's truth. Hence the message in the story of Shadrach, Meschach, and Abednego. They stood up to their king and government, even if their stand would cost them their lives. We are called to be set apart from the world, not to conform to it.

> We stand for truth, not to fight others
> but to show the world that our faith is not
> fragile and it won't crumble,
> no matter what comes along.

I hope and pray that these words will find their way into the hands of church leaders who will recognize that this apathy is the most crucial issue among the leadership of our churches. The Bible states clearly Jesus' words in Revelation 3:15-16, and they apply to individuals as well as to the church and its leaders: "I know all the things you do, that you are neither hot nor cold. I wish that you were one or the other! But since you are like lukewarm water, neither hot nor cold, I will spit you out of my mouth!"

Some seminaries teach a theology that omits punishment for unrepented sin. That does not excuse pastors for failing to warn. Pastors, leaders, and the church are all accountable for calling out sin and warning of its consequences.

If I've raised the ire of those who disagree, it was intentional.

Corporate culture is the only sustainable competitive advantage that is completely within the control of the entrepreneur. Develop a strong corporate culture first and foremost.

—David Cummings

Chapter 3

Culture in the Workplace

Back when companies shared their success stories as a way of giving back to other businesses, I had the opportunity to attend a seminar put on by the Ritz-Carlton. It was very interesting to learn how their fanatical customer service had made them an icon in the hospitality industry.

First of all, Ritz-Carlton trained their employees on the what and why of their standards and core values. Then they gave each employee ownership in the company. Not monetary ownership but rather the right to take care of any issue that their guests might have. Employees were then encouraged to go above and beyond what the customer would expect. Each individual was given a dollar amount that they could use to satisfy any shortfalls the company had incurred related to their guest's experience. It was called "The $2,000 Rule." Any employee could, without having to ask a manager, spend up to $2,000 to rescue the guest's experience.

The seminar explained in detail how employees were trained. From the minute their guests walked into the building, the culture Ritz-Carlton had established kicked in. They asked their guests what their favorite wine was and what newspaper they preferred, and from that day forward, that particular guest could walk into any Ritz-Carlton in the country and find their favorite beverage and specific newspaper of choice waiting for them when they entered their room. Business travelers were asked to set out the suit, tie, and shirt they would be wearing the next day, and the hotel made sure it was professionally ironed and ready to wear. Everything guests asked for was done with excellence. If they needed transportation to the airport or some other destination, a cab driver would be waiting at the appropriate time. The list of things the hotel did for their guests was quite unheard of. I do not know if they still continue all of those practices, but in today's world of poor customer service, it would be a breath of fresh air.

Ritz-Carlton had developed a culture that delighted even the most discerning guest. They were intentional in how their people were to interact with their guests, and their employees were empowered to give the customers what they needed. At that time, Ritz-Carlton also owned the Marriott chain of hotels, and I asked the speaker if the employees at the Ritz-Carlton were paid more for providing first-class service than they would be at the Marriott, where the standards were different. The pay was the same at both hotels, but with very different results. Why? Because the Ritz employees felt and acted like owners of the hotel.

The culture of any business starts on the top rung and depends on how we as leaders demonstrate the standards through our own actions. In the profound words of John Maxwell, "Everything rises and falls on leadership." The reason this principle is not taken more seriously in the business world is twofold.

First, it is hard to put a dollar number on the value of a vibrant culture when other things are vying for our time and money. It's very difficult to attract good candidates to hire, and harder yet to retain good, well-trained people. The value that a good culture brings is hard to put on a financial statement in terms of real dollars generated by a character and culture program. Such a program is not a short-term fix, but rather a lifetime of teaching and modeling the character around which you desire to form the culture.

Second, in the process of teaching great character, leaders of our companies—starting with the CEO first and then all the rest of the executive team—must especially embody great character. Character-built culture starts with the top leader and filters down to everyone in any role in the company. When core values are instilled in all of the leadership team of any organization, then and only then will there be a total buy-in to the great culture they have initiated. This forward momentum will become unstoppable, and competitors will be left to wonder how such a company does what they do.

One of my most admired leadership authors, Peter Drucker, says that "Culture eats strategy for breakfast." This begs the question, Why isn't a great culture then at the top of most companies' values statement? Because transforming results by changing beliefs and behaviors, as Drucker put it, is easier said than done. Actually, it's a daunting task to change people's beliefs and behaviors; it's next to impossible, especially in a diverse company that has people from many walks of life who have learned what right and wrong means to them and who are usually deeply rooted in their beliefs, be they right or wrong. If you employ one hundred people, chances are you will have about that many ideas on what your people think the culture should be.

It's not as complicated as you might think, but it takes commitment, perseverance, and most of all, owners, CEOs, managers, and supervisors who are committed to being the people we want the rest of our team to emulate. Once all of management has bought into our desired culture, the rest becomes easier. This procedure is a top-down way of influencing our people, and the culture becomes very contagious. The vast majority of our people will love the results they are helping to generate, and the holdouts will either become acclimated to the new culture or they will leave.

But I have never seen or heard of anyone wanting to leave a place with great culture. I have found that when companies take good care of their people, those people will take good care of your customers.

ᘓ♦ᘕ

High-performing teams have good and cohesive relationships. Any great team begins with the relationship between the team and their boss, and it is really up to the boss to determine what that relationship looks like.

> Teamwork makes the dream work,
> but a vision becomes a nightmare
> when the leader has a big dream and a bad team.
> —John Maxwell

Step one is for the boss to clearly communicate all expectations, such as the daily schedule, priority tasks, and work flow. This step is crucial in any type of job environment. Many times—and unfortunately—a company offers a sugarcoated version of expectations in order to make the hire. Instead, just tell it like it is; the best surprise is no surprise. After the hire, the boss or HR person will need to do an in-depth training and orientation meeting where expectations are defined more clearly. This is the company's first opportunity to introduce and demonstrate the culture and how it will affect the employee's growth and future opportunities.

In my days as CEO, one of the tasks I personally took on was the orientation for new hires. I wanted them all to hear directly from me how and why we had the culture we have. I believe this explanation is not the job of our HR person but should come from the president of the company. The HR person would also be present to go over all the employment benefits and other information a new hire needed to know.

One of the tasks I gave new hires was to think about the culture of the company where they had worked previously. Was it good, bad, or just not intentional? I asked them to leave their old culture, whether good or bad, by the door as they walked into our company and focus on adopting our culture. I explained to them how important it was for everyone to embrace our culture as it was established by me, the owner and CEO. And if I could go back to those days and do the hiring all over again, I would put together a little one-page contract. It would list ten to twelve things their jobs would entail; and on the back side, I'd list the things we always do to preserve our culture. I would then have new hires sign and date the contract, give them a copy, and make sure they knew that we would hold them accountable for what they had just signed. That may sound pretty stringent, because it probably is. But as I said, the best surprise is no surprise, both for the new hire and for the company.

An employee's first week should be a great experience, not a frightening one. They can be paired with a helper who will show them what to do and how to do it; then they're given a chance to try it with someone by their side. A new employee's work environment should be a friendly place. To be accepted and helped or trained by friendly people makes a great first impression and fosters good relationships from day one. Even though supervisors and managers will guide new hires, if fellow employees also help them and answer questions, great results will follow.

A strong team needs solid relationships because it will be tested during extra-busy times, or when people are out sick, or when an employee has a family emergency. That's when good work relationships kick in and everyone is willing to go the extra mile to cover for the missing person.

A leadership group may consist of managers, supervisors, the executive team and/or a CEO. Even though these people all have different responsibilities, they should look out for each other and make sure nothing falls through the cracks. To have a seasoned and well-trained senior leadership team that has longevity is priceless. Turnover at this level is extremely disruptive, so the relationships at this level are critical.

In order for the company structure to operate smoothly, titles and positions for all levels of management are needed. These titles and positions are never to be used to coerce or threaten people by the power that comes with them, but rather to influence others to carry out the wishes of the CEO. That is the job of everyone within the company. The CEO carries out the wishes of the shareholders. (That is, if they are ethical.)

When all levels of leadership and their teams work in unison, it becomes a thing of great beauty as well as an unstoppable force. The company that can achieve this will be the greatest nightmare of their competitors with bad culture.

Great culture in a company is like a finely-tuned guitar or violin. If one of the six strings on a guitar is loose or broken, the sound it produces is off key and flawed, so that even the best artist can't produce the quality of music that the instrument is capable of. This is also true when a team member is out of step with the culture. It affects the whole team or department, and if left unchecked, the discord will spread like a cancer.

This situation is really the acid test for anybody in leadership. When all the necessary warnings and chances for a change in behavior have been exhausted, and the only option is to let the employee go, we need to step up to the plate and terminate their employment. No matter how valuable the person's contribution is to the company, if we really value the culture and our reputation, we need to take action. To tolerate poor character and behavior that doesn't meet our standards erodes the culture and causes good people to lose respect for leadership. Taking decisive action is the only way to keep our culture clean, and it sends a strong message that we will never tolerate poor character.

In the long-term, money will never fix a bad-culture company. High turnover is always the result of a company with a bad culture. All things being equal and compensation and benefits notwithstanding, companies with great-culture reputations will win the battle of attracting the best job seekers. That's why I assign relationships the utmost importance in a company's culture. It is easier to leave a job when there are no great relationships also being left behind, but it's much more difficult to turn your back on a job where you get to work with friends.

Watching a football game between the Cincinnati Bengals and the Buffalo Bills, I saw an excellent example of a cohesive team at work. During the first quarter of the game, Damar Hamlin of the Bills had completed a play, and after the tackle, he stood up and then immediately collapsed onto the field. Damar had suffered a cardiac arrest. The medics and an ambulance were brought out and were all gathered around him. They performed CPR and then loaded him into the ambulance and transported him to the hospital.

Damar has thankfully made a full recovery, and the incident has served as a statement to millions of viewers who were watching the game. The power of prayer was on full display during the near-death experience, as well as later, after his recovery. The Lord works in mysterious ways. The scene that followed his heart attack was like none I've ever seen before. All of the Bills team, coaches, and staff gathered in a circle out on the corner of the field and knelt down and prayed for their fallen comrade. You could have heard a pin drop in the enormous stadium packed with thousands of people. In that moment, many people bowed their heads in support and prayed as well.

It was obvious that this was a cohesive team and that they loved their teammate. They were very concerned about his well-being, and with tears streaming down their faces they prayed to Almighty God to bring healing to Damar. The opposing team was equally distraught and in prayer for him. The sight will not soon be forgotten. This played out on national television, and the game was suspended. As the somber fans filed out of the stadium, the scene was quite dramatic. These two teams are at the top of the NFL standings, and it was very evident that they are closely knit. It was a profound example of good culture.

Recently I met with Reinhard Klett, who had read my book, *Business With a Higher Purpose,* and had sent me a copy of his own book, *Letting Go Saved My Life.* We had a delightful visit and compared our life experiences and leadership stories.

Reinhard came from Germany and had spent some time working at Mercedes-Benz as an engineer, so I was immediately drawn into a conversation about German-engineered cars. I asked him how it is that the German cars feel different in their ride, the performance is better, and still they beat our American cars in gas mileage. It seems to me that if I were one of the big three car manufacturers in the US, I would simply buy these German-made vehicles, take them apart piece by piece to find out why the power-versus-mileage secret exists, and simply use their engineering in our own cars. His answer was profound. He said that there are few noticeable differences in the way the engine parts, the drivetrain, and the suspension look. But over many years, their machined parts have been made to the most exacting tolerances to avoid any friction that would cause heat or wear and tear and therefore take more power to run the vehicle. It is not a matter of one or two major differences, but many small, almost unnoticeable differences that in the end add up to big differences.

So it is with companies. It is the little tweaks, teaching, coaching, and leadership that keep the friction to a minimum and let the company run smoothly and in perfect harmony for its people—who, by the way, are the engine and drivetrain and suspension of any company. Strong relationships provide protection from a multitude of deadly sins in any organization, and those relationships don't happen on their own.

Every CEO is in fact a Chief Cultural Officer. The terrifying thing is it's the CEO's actual behavior, not their speeches or list of core values they have put up on posters, that defines what the culture is. Without these four powers (Hiring, Firing, Promoting, Punishing), any employee at the company is along for the ride in a culture driven by someone more powerful than they are.

—Scott Berkun

Chapter 4

The Culture-Driven Leader

Behind every great culture there is a great leader. Be it in the home, the workplace, the government, or any other organization, the true leader sets the culture.

It is important to know that not every designated leader is actually the most influential person. In the home, the God-ordained leader is the man, but if he doesn't carry out his responsibilities, the wife has no choice but to do the job her husband should be doing. The same is true in business and all other organizations. The CEO or president should wield the most influence, but if they are weak, absent, or hide in their office, someone else will be the main influencer. I use the word "influencer" here because influence is really the factor that determines whether someone is actually the leader or just has a title.

The dictionary defines "influence" as "the power or capacity of causing an effect in indirect or intangible ways. The act or power of producing an effect, without apparent exertion of force, or direct exercise of command." So if you need to reinforce or emphasize your position in order to bring about results, you are leading by force and intimidation instead of influence. For example, if a child asks his father, "Why can't I do this?" and the answer is "Because I am your dad (or boss) and I say so," that's the wrong answer. Compliance that is forced upon someone without a viable reason is not received gladly or willingly. As a father, the right answer should be, "Because I love you too much to allow you to do something that could bring harm to you now or later on." As a boss, explaining the why is important. It could simply be that someone's actions are counterculture to what the company's core values are, but an explanation helps the person understand the boss's reasoning. That is the difference between an influential leader or someone who simply leads by their position.

The "Why?" has always been a teachable moment for me. Sometimes, a person really did not know the why, and other times, an employee was just pushing back to see if they could get a rise out of me. More often than not, the questions coming at me were on quality issues and manufacturing procedures. Most of my answers were based on practices and quality measures that my dad had established during his time leading the company. He usually had a very good reason for doing what he did, his knowledge and experience coming from a lifetime spent in the leather industry. His skill and foresight helped to make Weaver Leather what it is today. However, sometimes my explanation of the why wasn't sufficient for the perfectionist who worked in our Finish Department. She would reject perfectly good products that had only a small imperfection in the leather. One day, the reject pile got the best of me, and I went over to her work area and gently reminded her that leather is an imperfect material and our quality standards were exactly what I said they were. That seemed to do the trick, and we had no problems after that.

༄♦༄

The choice of a leader in a company or as a life partner will have long-term rewards or consequences. Choose either one with great care and deliberation. In both cases, emotions are not enough to go on. Find out if your core values match up with those of a potential life partner. In the search for a workplace leader, hire slowly with deliberation, and look for signs both good and bad.

The first attribute to look for is humility. Remember that you are deciding on what will shape your business or your home. Throughout the Bible we are taught the benefits of humility and warned of the downfall of the proud. Humility covers a multitude of sins, literally. When a person messes up, as we all do, are they quick to realize their failure and make amends, or does pride kick in and look for excuses or shift the blame elsewhere? What is your proposed leader or partner's reaction when someone questions a decision? Do they get angry or insulted? The person who defends a poor decision is a proud person, and in many cases is actually suffering from low self-esteem. The admission of an error can further lower their self-esteem. This person will thrive on being right and proving other people wrong. Many times, these people attempt to win the battle or the argument by bringing up others' faults and comparing others' accomplishments to their own. Humble people, on the other hand, do not seek recognition for their success but rather defer the credit to those who took the original idea or concept and made it more than they themselves might have seen possible.

The greatest example of true humility was exhibited by a man named Jesus, born out of wedlock (as many would be quick to point out) to a young virgin. Even though Jesus was born into a noble lineage of a long line of kings that went back to King David, His family was far from royalty. Joseph, Jesus' earthly father, was a humble carpenter. What was so amazing is that at the age of twelve Jesus already knew who He was, yet He continued to live like most kids did at the time. He worked with His father as a carpenter, and it wasn't until the age of thirty that He began His ministry of teaching and preaching.

He was king of kings and lord of lords, but He lived a human life here and regularly associated with the lowest of the low. He had the power to do many things that would get Him noticed and He performed many miracles that astounded people, but He always credited His power to raise the dead and heal the sick to His Heavenly Father who had given Him these gifts. The politicians and religious leaders of Jesus' day hated Him with a passion. He was a threat to their power and influence, and people were leaving their religious circles and following the man who knew all things. Those jealous leaders ended up killing Jesus. And although He had the power to stop His execution, He willingly gave himself as a sacrifice. That is why He is referred to as the Lamb of God. Sheep are defenseless and were used back in those days for sacrifices to God. He was killed, murdered in the most cruel and degrading way possible. The next time He visits the earth, He will come not as a Lamb but as the true king of kings.

I don't know of anyone, myself included, who could do what Jesus did and still be without a single sin in his lifetime here on Earth. He was our perfect example of living with humility. We have a ten-year-old grandson who is vibrant, energetic, and a competent little athlete. He has no reservations about telling me when he hits home runs or is one of the top three hitters on their All-Star team. It is our natural instinct to want to be recognized for a job well done. Even though we can never match Jesus' example, we are still called to be humble and not proud or boastful.

As leaders, we can make lots of demands that are self-serving. That's why humility is such a game changer. We can make public all the great things we have accomplished, we can associate with people who have fame and fortune, but the true acid test of who we are is our ability—or lack of it—to relate to and have a close relationship with anyone, like Jesus did.

Let's look at the opposite kind of leaders, a type that is found in many large corporations and publicly traded companies. Their salaries are seven or eight figures with packages that include stock options and bonuses for reaching the high goals of the board of directors. They answer to the chairman of the board, and the only real objectives are to hit the numbers by any means necessary. I am not saying there are no good leaders in Fortune 500 companies, but the culture in many of these companies takes a back seat to the almighty dollar. The money at stake can corrupt even the best of leaders if they are not firmly grounded in Christian values. This is just one of the reasons that financial goals are reached by doing things right, including having a great culture and a motivated, high-performance workforce. This is what the Bible says about this subject of striving for money only:

> For the love of money is the root of all evil. And some people craving money have wandered far from the true faith and pierced themselves with many sorrows. (1 Timothy 6:10)

Money is a great servant, but a terrible master. Show me a leader that is obsessed with money and wealth, and I will show you a proud, cunning, and sometimes ruthless leader who sees his workforce simply as a means to an end.

Whether our influence (and thus, our leadership) is in our business, church, family, social club, or any other network, we can use the following actions and attitudes as our humility checklist.

1. **Lead by helping others succeed**. The choice is always between doing it yourself or having someone on your team do it and get the credit for it and thus grow. The vast majority of people tend to let others know about their accomplishments in life and not give credit to other teammates or people who, in many cases, set up the winning touchdown. Helping others to succeed and grow is learned behavior, and it is one of the biggest game changers in business. It is the only way to grow good leaders in the company. It's this simple: when someone comes to you and compliments you about a great idea or decision, redirect that to your supporting staff and simply say, "Thank you! I would love to take the credit, but [name] is the one responsible for this. I will certainly relay this to her today." This is the high-protein food that grows leaders. It is easy, it is free, and it will ensure that you won't have to go outside the company to hire leaders who someone else has promoted.
2. **Lead courageously**. Leaders need to lead with courage and act. Humility is not weakness; it is confidence and determination devoid of pride. With inner strength, we won't throw in the towel just because things don't go as we planned. We need to be quick to innovate and find new and better ways to accomplish the goal. And (going back to #1) many times, getting others involved in solving a problem is a great way to both find the answer and honor the person who had the great solution. Remember, none of us are as good as all of us.

3. **Readily admit to mistakes**. When you blow it, admit it! Everyone already knows, so beat them to the punch by letting people know that you accept full responsibility. That's called accountability. How can we ever expect accountability from our team members if we ourselves are not accountable? This is also a large part of being a successful parent. An admission of wrongdoing is the fastest way to gain influence. How often does your boss admit mistakes or apologize for something they said? How often have you gone back to ask your kid for forgiveness? In my first 19 years while living with my parents, I never heard my dad apologize to us kids or to Mom. That was one of the reasons why he had so little influence on us. It was all about force, "My way or the highway."
4. **Seek advice and counsel from others**. The fastest way to reach your goals is to ask someone who has gone this way before you. For many, they have not because they ask not. To ask someone for advice is wise; to not ask someone in the know is often the action of pride. Thankfully, asking for advice is something that was modeled for me by my dad. I liked what I saw, and I followed his footsteps by asking credible advisers for their input.
5. **Have a high degree of self-awareness**. Knowing who we are, both what we're good at and what we aren't, is very important. I have found that whatever frustrates me is often someone else's strength, and they will do a better job than I could in half the time and get it right the first time. This is also the first step in being an accomplished delegator. Do you know what you're good at? Do you know what you do that you're really terrible at? If not, ask someone else on

your team. They know and will usually be happy to give you the answer!

6. **Be sincere and have clear motives**. It doesn't take people long to spot a phony. When we say one thing and mean another, our leadership comes into question. The only place that this is an acceptable way of leading is in our nation's capital. By the way, that's not meant to be funny—it is dead serious and it's why our country is in the greatest decline we've experienced since it's founding. Insincerity is a lie with a suit and a tie. It looks like high-powered politicians. I looked up the definition of a politician, and this is one: "A person who acts in a manipulative and devious way, typically to gain advancement within an organization." Bull's-eye!
7. **Treat everyone with kindness and respect**. This is an excellent test when looking for someone's true personality. We had a system worked out at our business. When people came to see me, the receptionist would call and tell me who was there. She would then have someone else show the visitor back to my office, which was a little ways from the main entrance. If the visitor was rude or demeaning, she would give me a quick call back and tell me that the guy was a jerk. This helped me make a good decision as to whether we should be buying their products or services.

Humility is a first big step into creating a great culture in companies. Face it, the culture in our homes and our businesses is not what we *say* it is—it is *who we are*. In both the workplace and the home, more is caught than taught. Whenever the leader is proud and arrogant, they and the people they lead produce a culture that reflects that. When an irate customer calls in and is unhappy about a shipment they received or demands to know where their order is, the customer service representative will become defensive and kill the relationship. That's the pride and the culture they have seen their CEO model. The employee from a culture of humility will want to serve their customers, and will go out of their way to satisfy the unhappy customer.

As parents, we are called to love our children and teach them right from wrong. And as Christ followers, our responsibility goes much deeper than that. We need to live our lives in such a way that we represent Jesus well. That's easier said than done, and we as parents sometimes deviate from this; then we need to let them know we were remiss or negligent in what we did or said that is counter to the culture we want to nurture in our home. Our influence as parents is paramount. It is not the church's job to teach and train our kids. It is not the school's job to teach them character. It is the parents' job. It doesn't "take a village," Hillary. It takes responsible parents who lead their children to become Christ followers.

On our own, we often struggle as we try to be great examples to our families and coworkers. It seems that the harder we try, the more difficult it is. We were born into this world not as little saints but as little sinners. No one had to teach us how to lie, cheat, steal, get angry, hit someone, or choose a life of crime. And that is called human nature. Much of who we are and what we do is also generational. What we have learned as children—from parents also struggling with human nature—is hard to shake as we get older. We were born with a sinful nature and into a sinful world. The only solution for sin is Jesus Christ.

ℵ♦ℑ

As a business owner, I made my company my mission and my ministry. Thirty years ago we started on a character journey in our workplace. After some years, I developed our own program, Lodestar Guidance.

The program presents 48 character principles and takes an in-depth look at each one and how it affects us if we follow the principle or the negative results of not following the principle. One character principle is featured in an all-employees meeting each month. Everyone at Weaver Leather, over 300 employees, would together watch the video that accompanies each principle. After the video, I expounded on the featured principle for that month. Each attendee was given a bulletin on that particular principle to read, study, and take home. We used this time to thoroughly explain the character principle and demonstrate how that attribute would affect not just our careers but our lives in general. We recognized people for displaying these traits in our own workplace.

At the monthly meeting, we not only shared and taught the principle of the month but also recognized and rewarded people for personifying the principle. This meeting was also a perfect platform for sharing with everyone what's happening inside the company, such as whether or not we reached our sales goals for the past month and how we are tracking toward our performance goals. We let everyone know what's coming up that's new and that we will need all hands on deck to make the venture a success. The meeting lasted about 30-40 minutes and I believe it was the most important thing we did monthly.

What this program has done for us as a company is hard to describe, but in short, it has over these many years developed a culture that very few companies could even dream of.

This is not the only culture guide, but what I do know is that if someone would choose to study and implement all 48 of these principles and spend one week on each one and then live out what they've learned, they would become dynamic culture leaders.

I used to believe that culture was "soft," and had little bearing on our bottom line. What I believe today is that our culture has everything to do with our bottom line, now and into the future.

—Vern Dosch

Chapter 5

The Rewards of a Great Culture

Rewards are never free. They are always a result of something done that is **above average.** After all, average is expected. It's our culture of hard work, perseverance, and a commitment to excellence that earns us rewards.

Sometimes it's the intangibles in the home and the workplace that are very simple but powerful and create an above-average culture. Little things, like coming home from a tough day at work and instead of being grumpy, saying, "How was your day, honey?" Or to your kids, "How was your day at school?" To the customer on the phone at work, "Thank you for the nice order. It was great to hear your voice again." Or, if the customer is well known, asking how they have been; and if they tell you of health issues or other hardships, tell them you will pray for them; better yet, say a little prayer right then over the phone.

In the family, the husband and wife together create the culture because when we marry, we become as one. The efforts of only one parent or the other will never be as effective as a united husband-and-wife team. A divided team is sometimes worse than a one-parent home. The kids are confused by contradictions and inconsistencies and end up blaming both adults. But when there's continuity and aligned values, the rewards are many. Children are secure, there is happiness and love between family members, and the culture of the home is conducive to growth and maturity.

In such a family, children get a firm foundation on which to build their own future homes, and the chances of those families having a good culture are much higher. A great culture becomes a generational thing, and it's the best inheritance we can give our children. It's the gift that keeps on giving. What parents wouldn't be happy to see this taking place?

A great culture in the family also produces a life that is free of regrets. As we come to the end of our time on Earth and we say our final goodbye and know that we have done our best in raising a happy, well-grounded family that shares our faith and values, we can be sure we have lived a life of excellence that money couldn't buy.

As a matter of fact, many times money is the downfall of this model. When things are easy and we give our sons and daughters money they did not earn to buy things they don't need, we have taken away the incentive to earn, to strive, and to succeed. Inheritance was meant to be received after the parents die, and not during their wage-earning years. Buying kids their first car and helping them with their education (if they so choose) is a good thing. Aside from that, less is more in terms of giving them monetary gifts that they did not earn.

Gladys and I got married at the age of 19. We bought a house for $11,900. I grew up as a carpenter and was able to fix up the house and it became a cozy little home. We had managed to scrape up enough money to put a $1,000 down payment on the house, and when I went to the bank to borrow the rest of the money, the banker asked me if I could get my dad to co-sign the loan. I reluctantly asked Dad if he would, and he said no. He had no interest in ending up as owner of a house he didn't want. So I went back to the banker and assured him we were good for the money, and he gave us the loan. With very few resources but much blood, sweat, and tears, we increased the value to triple what we had paid for it four years prior. Needless to say, we were elated that our hard work had paid off. And by the way, I was making between $3 and $4 an hour, and Gladys made even less. Today as I look back and reflect on this time in our life, I am glad that Dad didn't co-sign the mortgage on the house even though he could have. Our "scratching with the chickens" was rewarded with the tripling of our money.

ꕤ

> The biggest reward we can have is loyal team members and loyal customers.
> You can't buy either one of these.
> You earn them.

The rewards for the great-culture company are profound, both in moral and in financial stability. At Weaver Leather, some of the things we did to create our culture may have seemed to have vague or intangible rewards, but the bottom line and the opportunities prove differently.

Good culture rewards a company with a motivated workforce. When people feel cared for and appreciated, there's a willingness to go the second mile and to do whatever it takes to help the company reach its goals. Motivated and happy teams produce much more than unmotivated, unhappy teams. This is a fact and can easily be proven when comparing companies. Buying companies with a poor culture and not bringing them in-house but leaving them at a remote location with the same leadership is a great way to lose money—and sleep.

A great culture in a business looks different than a great family culture because there are many people involved in a business and some of those people grew up in dysfunctional homes. Their hurts and hangups have resulted in scars they bring with them into the workplace. A great-culture company can make a difference in that it can be a healing place for hurting people, a place where caring people want to help their coworkers.

If the culture of a company includes a Christian-led leadership team, the workplace is seen as a ministry. After all, we often spend more working hours at our jobs than we spend in our homes. The company that is infused with biblical principles will have a profound effect on its unsaved people. As an employee, it's hard to dislike and disrespect those who love and care about you and your soul. And when things get tough in your life, to have someone who empathizes with you, prays for you, and has your best interest at heart will be the draw that you may need to help you change your life.

Being honest and open is always a great way to gain the confidence of your great people. Remember—the culture begins at the top! One of the ways we showed trust and confidence in our team members was to share as much information about the company as we could. Most companies do the exact opposite because they think the information will cause employees to be resentful and want to be paid more. But along with my long-time friend and accountant, we explained to all our people how our financial structure actually worked. A screen at the front of our meeting center had the top half of the screen filled with a giant dollar bill. So as our accountant detailed where all the money went, the dollar bill shrank with every cost and expenditure. Cost of goods might be 40 percent, operating cost might be another 20 percent, labor another 20 percent, and so on. And at the end, we had one dime left out of the dollar—and then taxes took a nickel of that. Our people were dumbfounded at how little was actually left of that dollar. The morning after the meeting, as I took my walk through the plant and offices, I made it a point to ask people what their estimate before the meeting was, in regards to our profits. The answers were quite enlightening. Some estimated we made 50 percent profit, some said 25 percent, and other various guesses. Aside from our executive team, no one had guessed our profit to be as small a percentage as it was.

Our people always knew that it was team members first and customers second. Have you ever heard someone say that "The customer comes first"? Or that the customer is always right? At Weaver Leather, that was not the case. Out of the thousands of customers we have, there is a small percentage who are irrational, convinced they are paying too much, looking for ways to buy for less, lodging complaints with every order, and the list of headaches goes on. When these customers crossed the line by being rude and profane to our customer service reps (CSRs) or they decided to not pay their bills, they were taken off our customer list and their accounts were closed. Losing good team members over such issues was far more costly than losing sales to a bad customer. By the way, in my 40 years, I only had to make this call to shut down accounts five or six times, and all but two of those customers came back and apologized for their rude and inappropriate behavior. Their accounts were then restored. The other two we never heard from again. Good riddance. Let some other company deal with those people.

When people take ownership in a company's success, they know that the better the company does, the greater will be their reward. Profit sharing is step one in a great leader's way to be more than just a boss but now a partner in sharing the company's bounty. I have always believed that generosity starts with the people who have given us their best efforts for extended periods of time.

Over the years, we have always printed a monthly newsletter for all team members and our sales reps. It had the latest news of significant events and news from our team members such as new employees and additions to families. Along with in-house news, we would include the comments our customers sent along with their payments. Their appreciation for outstanding customer service was mentioned often, along with comments on the friendly reps, in-house salespeople, and all they came in contact with. These testimonials were the encouragement we all needed to strive for excellence.

Another idea that was designed to get people involved in our value of giving was to set up a benevolence fund where both team members and the company contributed. When a big need came up and someone or a family member was suffering a hardship, the funds would be used to help them financially during those times. This did two things: it let our people know we cared about them and their families, and it gave them a chance to give generously to help in the case of another team member's misfortune. All rewards are the result of sowing seeds along the way. Like the farmer's crop, the seeds sown take time to germinate and then grow, but in 90 to 120 days, the kernel of corn planted will produce 800 kernels on one ear of corn. That's the ratio for generosity as well. In due time, our generous giving will produce a bountiful harvest. Generosity starts with a giving mindset, that transcends what most people think is fair.

In a great-culture business, team members become ambassadors for hiring great people. Over the years, Weaver Leather has given a little cash "finder's fee" when a team member recommends a person for employment. Very few people will recommend we hire a person if that employee himself is unhappy with the culture. It is also a fact that people rarely recommend potential hires that have bad character. In the end, a poor hire reflects badly on the one who recommended them.

༻•༺

Customer loyalty to the great-culture company is another reward. The culture of a company is rarely hidden, and customers love great service and happy customer care.

I've retired. But I realize that today's business climate is unlike anything I have ever seen. "Customer service" is a thing of the past.

Lead times are measured in months, not days. Phone calls are not returned, and employers are lowering their standards just to attract warm bodies. There are three jobs available for every good and qualified employee. In my opinion, this has caused many business owners and CEOs to lower their standards of quality and service to a level that would have been unheard of just three or four years ago.

For a business, going the extra mile is uncommon. Today, the mentality is the "get all you can, can all you get, and sit on the lid" mindset. It's the thinking that if you the customer wins, I the supplier must have lost. I know many businesses take that approach, but it's the easiest way to lose a customer. It's not just hard currency that matters, it's how the customer feels when the transaction is made.

How the customer feels starts with the person who answers the phone—oops, that's a rarity these days. Now automated attendants give you many choices and then you push the right key on your phone and get put on hold or a waiting list. One of our salespeople was at a trade show and upon his return came into my office and said he had a great idea to make our customers' phone experience much more personal. He had talked to someone at the trade show who said their company's phone was answered by none other than the company's president. Even though it was a recording, their customers were thrilled to have the courtesy of the owner's voice on the greeting and menu. Needless to say, I recorded the welcome and menu on our phone system and thanked callers for their patronage. This little action, which took only a few minutes, brought us many positive comments from our customers. When I attended the one trade show each year that was the biggest and most attended, many people said hello and greeted me by my name, and I was clueless as to who they were. They would laugh and remind me that every time they called in to place an order, they were greeted by my voice and message.

Most of our orders came in by phone, and our CSRs would field hundreds of calls a day. I would dare to say that our ladies were some of the most professional and kindhearted of any company out there. We have a great leader in this department who sets the culture, and the results are excellent. When someone is on the other end of the phone and is unhappy with something, she will jump in and with her controlled, calm, and friendly voice, diffuse the situation and take care of the problem. That's leadership! Her willingness to do the job that most people would prefer to avoid gains her much favor with her staff.

Other reasons to buy from us included the pattern of excellent service and shipping 98 percent of our orders within 24 hours, along with our iron-clad guarantee of quality or your money back. This was what attracted new customers and kept our existing customers.

The biggest reward for going over and above and exceeding our customers' expectations was loyalty to our company and our brand. Our customers have many options on where to buy their products, and lots of lower-cost suppliers have tried to make inroads and get their business. The best thing that could and did happen was when our customer gave the "other" company an order just to test the waters. Usually the lead time on that order was not one to two days but two to three weeks. Strike one. The product's quality and "sales support" did not measure up. Strike two. And here's the biggee: The stores' customers loved our products. We had an easy money-back guarantee, and the final customers had become name brand loyal and wouldn't buy the replacement product. Strike three. The retailer's customer has the final say on what they buy, and that resonates with the store owner.

None of these attributes would have been possible without a culture that bought into our core values and fanatical customer care. The rewards came in the form of being #1 in a number of the industries we serve. We could sell at profitable prices that still allowed our dealers to make their margins because we went over and above the industry standards. Our influence spread to the end users as well, and it's hard not to carry products that retail customers ask for by name.

Our company's culture also affects our supply chain and our ability to serve our customers well. When people with good character are purchasing supplies, vendors also experience benefits of good culture. Good vendors are not easy to find and can do us a great deal of good in timely delivery and great quality products. To beat down a vendor on terms or pricing and concessions is detrimental to long-term relationships. Great, happy vendors make the clock tick smoothly in business.

Our sales reps in the field who call on the retailers also bought into the culture. They made good money on our line and have represented us very well over the years. Our standards are high, and not all of those reps were comfortable with our standards. In some instances they either left us for a competitor's lines or were asked to leave.

Great culture is only as good as our willingness to enforce our high standards and call out those who do not represent us well. A low tolerance for insubordination, both inside the company and among our outside reps, is key to keeping a culture unblemished. Failure to hold people accountable is the undoing of great businesses, families, or any organizations. It erodes the very culture and left unchecked will destroy a good reputation in a fraction of the time it took to build it.

Great rewards come from making good decisions that benefit our team members *and* our customers. These decisions are based on a win-win philosophy. If our company lowers product quality and thus lowers our cost and the customer buys the product at the same or higher price, we might win short-term, but the customer loses. And that doesn't work in the long run. The customer is ultimately in charge of the decision on who they'll buy from. If the customer wins and the company loses, we cut our own throat and will eventually fall on hard times. Our goal should always be to delight the customer with our products and services and to make it easy to buy from us.

Our economy is losing steam and inflation is heating up to levels I saw in 1980 when our fearless leader Jimmy Carter led our country to lows that we are going to be experiencing again. As demand is starting to dwindle, the great-culture and great-service companies will also feel the slowdown of the economic downturn that is approaching, but the first to go out of business are those businesses that have the worst customer service and/or products. The strong survive and thrive in those hard times and that is one of the rewards of choosing excellence. Customers will be quick to remember the good suppliers, and they'll also remember those who let them down when things were good. Our good deeds will be remembered and our bad ones as well.

When it comes to business, great products, great service, and friendly people—all of which represents great culture—will always win out in the end. It's the little things that will stand out, make our companies just a little different, and cause our customers to choose us instead of our competitors.

I also want to mention rewards that come from doing our best, then giving back to God no less than 10 percent of our profits.

Giving to causes and charities that not only help the poor, widows, and orphans but provide aid in the name of Jesus opens the doors for these charities to share why those gifts were given. The why is very simple: to fulfill the command that we were given by Jesus Himself. After Jesus was killed and rose from the dead on the third day, He appeared to His disciples and said this:

> "Therefore, go and make disciples of all nations, baptizing them in the name of the Father and the Son and the Holy Spirit. Teach these new disciples to obey all my commands I have given you. And be sure of this: I am with you always, even to the end of the age." Matthew 28:19-22

In order for people to go and fulfill the Great Commission, someone must send them, and that's where we come into play. Without our generosity, these ministries cannot bring food, fresh water systems, and medical care and certainly cannot deliver this message of the Gospel. That is why our best efforts plus God's favor on us complete the circle of working hard and giving back a portion to the Kingdom of God.

In 1980 when our country went through the worst recession of my life, I was in the building business. With prime interest rates at more than 20 percent, new home sales had been stopped dead, and our little construction business came to its demise. My dad had started up a leather manufacturing business that was in its seventh year, and he asked my help to continue to grow it and manage it. I consented, but with grave reservations because Dad and I had a very strained relationship. To say that it was "strained" was stating it mildly. We had very little communication with each other, so I was surprised when I got a phone call and he asked if I had any interest in getting involved in the leather manufacturing business. With no other options, I agreed to make the move and to put the building business behind me.

As I worked hard to learn the trade and the business, it started to grow, and it seemed to be on a good track for becoming a good little business. Then, very unexpectedly, Dad died in an instant. I was left with quite a few areas of the business in which I still leaned on his many years of experience to bring clarity to my questions.

Dad's death became the crucible that forced me to depend on God for the future of the company. What I did have was a young man who had worked with Dad most of the seven years of the company. Myron Stutzman, our production manager, was well trained and experienced in all of manufacturing, and he was the bridge we needed to keep growing, develop products, and lead the production team.

However, the thought of going through another near-bankruptcy left me feeling vulnerable. It was at that point that my life changed in a big way. I asked God for wisdom and leadership and to supply our needs in terms of finding the right people we would need to grow the company and take it to a much higher level. When I prayed that prayer, I ended it with a promise to God that if He would supply the needs I had asked for in my prayer, I would from that day forward invest no less that 10 percent of our earnings to further His kingdom. I promised that I would do that for as long as I had breath to live.

That was the beginning of our real success. We were able to hire the people we needed at the time we needed them, and many of those people are still in place and doing phenomenal jobs at what they do. Without these people, we could not have experienced the growth we did over the next 40 years. This included sales reps and management leaders, and most of these people came to us without any prompting from us or help-wanted ads. They simply walked in and asked to become part of our company.

Early on, my vision for the company was to have excellence in everything we do, from keeping our facility clean and neat, to producing only top-quality products, to developing a culture that produced a workplace where our people could thrive. When we did that, it attracted people with good character in leadership, production, and all departments of the company. This gave us depth and people we could promote into leadership positions. We were not forced to go outside for every position we needed to fill in top management.

So in summary, over the years God did over and above what I asked Him for that morning I prayed that fervent prayer. Today we employ over 350 people and produce and sell more in one morning than we did in a whole year 40 years ago. Not only were my prayers answered, but I never dreamed how God's blessings and favor would impact our destiny. My promise to give back 10 percent of everything we earned did not waver. I have no doubt that our willingness to trust God to provide us with the 90 percent so we could give His 10 percent was a key factor. After all, the promise He gave us in the Bible is quite specific. These are Jesus' words in Luke 6:38:

> "Give and you will receive. Your gift will return to you in full—pressed down, shaken together to make room for more, running over and poured into your lap. The amount you give will determine the amount you get back."

He even asks us to "put him to the test" in Malachi 3:10:

> "Bring all the tithes into the storehouse so there will be enough food in my temple. If you do," says the LORD of Heaven's Armies, "I will open the windows of heaven for you. I will pour out a blessing so great you won't have room to take it in! Try it! Put me to the test!"

If this is not an iron-clad guarantee, then what is? So for those who believe that our businesses are exempt from this giving principle, **I challenge you to try it** and put Him to the test.

There are scores of people waiting for someone just like us to come along; people who will appreciate our compassion, our encouragement, who will need our unique talents. Someone who will live a happier life merely because we took the time to share what we had to give.

—Leo Buscaglia

Chapter 6

Multiplying Our Gifts and Talents

Almighty God created us in His image. He is perfect in every way; we, on the other hand, are not perfect. He has, though, given each of us special gifts and talents to use to live out our lives with excellence. He also gave us free choice, which means we have choices in what we do with those gifts, whether we leave their potential untapped or develop them into excellence. I firmly believe that **our earthly and eternal rewards are founded on how we make use of what we've been given.**

Reasons for not reaching our full potential can be varied. Some people are born into poverty. Some are born and raised in such bad environments and culture that they never recover. But for most people, multiplying their God-given abilities is dependent on making good choices during their lifetime.

Now, all of us make poor choices along our life journey that we live to regret, but normally we can still change course and go down better roads if we are honest with ourselves, take inventory of the tight spots we get into, and realize that we have met the enemy and it is us. To recognize our failures and then continue after adjusting our direction is many times what brings us success.

We all struggle with hurdles and roadblocks that pop up on our journey and can trip us up and cause us to not reach our full potential. And now I'm not talking about economic, environmental, or cultural factors. These are challenges that arise within. As we face each of these, we have a choice in how we respond. The top five difficulties that hold us back are these:

1) Doubt. We doubt our own ability to fulfill and achieve the goals we have set. Most doubt stems from fear, and fear is a byproduct of insecurity. As parents or leaders in the workplace, we can play a big role in building the confidence of our children or the people we lead. When we observe our son's or daughter's actions and achievements, we can compliment them on a job well done and let them know they are good at what they do. In the workplace, it is our job as leaders to spot people's gifts and talents, then let them know you noticed and encourage them to use their giftedness even more. That's the way to promote people: seeing them do something with excellence, encouraging them, and then having them grow and flourish in that field. This will develop great leaders from within. It's amazing what a little honest affirmation does to people. It gives them courage to do more and the desire to please you with the results.

Let me give you an example. Growing up, I didn't hear much affirmation from my dad, but working with him the last day before his death (which came as a shock to me because of its suddenness), he told me that for the past three years he had watched me lead the little company he had started seven years before, and he saw I had dynamic leadership skills and talents. Needless to say, I was astounded at this compliment and remember that moment of nearly 40 years ago as if it were yesterday. So be kind, and let someone know their talents are noted and appreciated.

2) Procrastination. We wait for someone else to get the ball rolling and don't take responsibility to just do it. Procrastination is the greatest enemy of excellence and achievement. (More on this dangerous—even fatal—habit in Chapter 12.)

3) Bitterness. Somebody wrongs or hurts us, and we play the blame game and become bitter. This will stop all forward motion. We stay in a rut. Our pastor gave us a word picture for this: That rut is really a grave with both ends kicked out. So it's best to forgive and forget and get on with pursuing our goals.

4) Lack of courage. We can lose our courage, and when our courage is lost, so is our perseverance, and all our enthusiasm drains away. Hence the dream dies. Many times, this loss of courage is simply a byproduct of fatigue. When we are tired, our problems loom larger. It's always better not to make decisions when we are in this frame of mind. The old saying is that fatigue makes cowards out of all of us.

5) Worry. Along our way, we all come face-to-face with issues for which we have no quick answer. Worry sets in, and prolonged worry causes stress, and stress left unchecked can cause depression. The Bible has the best prescription for this, found in Philippians 4:6-7:

> Do not be anxious about anything, but in every situation, by prayer and petition, with thanksgiving, bring your request to God. And the peace of God, which transcends all understanding, will guard your hearts and your minds in Christ Jesus.

Almost all great people who have been real difference-makers in our country or world had real hardships and made many mistakes along the way. They undoubtedly faced most if not all of these five hurdles. It seems that hardships and setbacks are a part of producing excellence in a person. Difficulty tests our resolve and makes us stronger. Challenges refine our character.

Over the past thirteen years, I have had eight surgeries, and I'm about to have Number Nine. The recovery and therapy along with pain and sleepless nights have taken a toll on my body and spirit. But what I have found is that we rarely make the needed changes in our lives during good times; change and growth come in the valleys of our lives. I don't understand that part of our human psyche, but it seems like we draw nearer to God because we need His help in these times.

The most notable example of this was the apostle Paul. He not only had a chronic ailment that bothered him, but in his lifetime, he endured hardships that were brutal. Anyone with less zeal and devotion to their cause would have thrown in the towel. He was kidnapped, beaten, threatened, arrested many times, accused in lawsuits, interrogated, ridiculed, ignored, shipwrecked, bitten by a poisonous snake, and then… executed. He never gave up and was one of the most influential writers of the Bible. (He wrote that prescription for worry in Philippians 4.) Out of the 27 books of the New Testament, Paul wrote 13 or 14 of them. He is known as the great encourager of the churches he had planted, and he asked for only his basic needs from his followers. The single word to describe him was *zealous.* Nothing could stop him in his quest for excellence. I am honored to share the same name he had, but fall way short of his work and example.

Our quest for excellence and multiplying our talents and gifts really has to begin with a keen sense of self-awareness and clearly knowing where and what our giftedness really is. Everyone I know who has experienced real and lasting success has done so in areas in which they are gifted. **Excellence will not be reached when we work in areas we're not gifted in.** It's hard enough to reach excellence when we're doing what we are gifted at.

Many people, if asked what their top strength areas are, would say, "I don't know." It's pretty hard to develop our gifts and talents if we're clueless about what they are. If you're serious about this and are interested in finding out where your skill set is, I would recommend finding someone who does the DISC test and is a consultant who can explain how your personality traits can be used to further your career and shape your future. We have used this and other tests in our workplace with great success. Finding a person whose skill set fits each job is a great way to form an excellent team in your workplace. Having your strengths match who you are and who God created you to be can change the outcome of your life. Along with the will to be the best one can be, having these strengths properly aligned with a job is what truly makes winners.

ꙮ♦ꙮ

No matter how dynamic our talents, everything can go down the drain if we lack character. Look at all the legacies that have been blemished by flawed character. I'm talking about going from the Hall of Fame to the Hall of Shame.

One of my favorite authors is Bill O'Reilly. With Martin Dugard, O'Reilly wrote the Killing Series of books and tapes. The latest one was *Killing the Legends: The Lethal Danger of Celebrity*. Names we all know met untimely deaths because they were consumed with their power and celebrity status. These were men known around the world for who they were and what they had accomplished: Elvis Presley, John Lennon, and Mohammed Ali. All were extremely talented in their careers. They were very wealthy and had anything and everything they could have wanted. That is, everything except accountability partners to keep them on the straight and narrow. Attempting to escape the masses of people who wanted to be seen with them, they became isolated, and a lack of character in isolation did them in. A word to the wise: If fame and fortune is what you long for, it's a really good sign that you shouldn't have it.

Many times the fame and fortune that someone achieves will go to their head and they feel they are invincible and the good life destroys them. The more success and fame people achieve, the more they need accountability partners in their lives. Someone who has their best interests at heart and is not afraid to speak into their life if they see danger signs. I have several people, including my wife, who will speak truth into my life and caution me when they see me doing something that goes against my spoken core values. They have been my friends for much of my life, and I treasure them.

The Bible says, "As iron sharpens iron, so a friend sharpens a friend" (Proverbs 27:17). The concept of "iron sharpening iron" implies that two pieces of iron are needed to sharpen either one. Left isolated, both blades would be dull and become useless. The writer of this verse was a king by the name of Solomon, known as the wisest man who ever lived. In all his wisdom, Solomon knew that God expects us to live and serve in community of other believers. He says in Proverbs 6:4, "Faithful are the wounds of a friend, but deceitful are the kisses of an enemy." This concept is proven to be true. It is better to accept godly advice or even constructive criticism from someone we know, someone we love, and someone we know cares about us than it is from a stranger or casual acquaintance. When someone has our best interests at heart and yet speaks words of correction that might hurt us or our pride, we can rest assured their counsel is sincere.

What makes these verses so powerful is that they were written by someone who violated this very principle and died a broken and bitter man. Solomon had it all in terms of wealth, power, and wisdom. In his own words, he said he had everything his heart desired. His downfall was that he had 900 wives and concubines, and some of these were heathen women who served foreign gods. They led him astray. He knew better, but my guess is no one had the guts to tell him where his life was headed.

If the wisest man who ever lived could be led astray, we certainly can as well. So stay connected with good people who will speak truth to you and then be humble and thank them for the advice they give you. No one is strong enough to successfully walk alone, so choose your friends carefully.

The most significant man to ever walk the face of this earth was Jesus. The masses of people wanted something from Him, and others wanted to kill Him. He died as a common criminal with two thieves by His side. He was only 33 years of age. Every time we date any document, we use His birth as a reference of time. He never wrote a book or held public office. But His life changed all those who chose to follow Him. It's our choice whether to do great things or to be famous. Choosing to follow this Man is the key.

ജ♦�cs

We have been using the phrase "gifts and talents." Let's clearly define the two—because they are not the same. Talents are inherited; gifts are received. All of us have inherited certain talents from our parents and passed down from generation to generation. Think about how often you have seen second- and third-generation doctors, pastors, athletes, and leaders. When I look at my Weaver family tree, quite a few similarities in talents appear among my cousins.

Gifts, on the other hand, are just that; they are "gifts" and gifts come from a giver. These are spiritual gifts that the Spirit of God gives us when we become born-again believers. Talents are possessed by the saved and unsaved, but only believers receive the gifts the Holy Spirit has for them. So we have an opportunity to go above and beyond our natural, inherited talents and have the gifts of the Spirit. These gifts are many, but here are some examples: the word of wisdom, the word of knowledge, faith (extraordinary trust and surrender), gifts of healing, preaching, the distinguishing of spirits, service, teaching, exhortation, giving, leadership, mercy, apostleship, evangelism, and pastoral care.

Some of the spiritual gifts may seem like they are natural talents. I know some dynamic non-Christian leaders who have accomplished much. **But a talented *and* gifted leader builds an organization that has a God-honoring culture,** promoting unity and strong commitment to the organization and what it stands for. Talents are developed and expected. Gifts are supernatural, given by our Creator to accentuate the talents we inherited.

When our talent becomes infused by the Holy Spirit of God, it goes to a new level that can be found only in believers. We can go over and above what our natural talents would have done for us, in ways that will amaze us and those we lead.

Leadership that is God-infused looks very, very different than leadership that is talent-based and given to us by our genealogy. That's where the "great" of "great culture" comes in. It's the unseen edge that your competition can't quite get their arms around; and even if they could, their core values differ greatly from core values that are God-based. Weaver Leather is an example of this scenario. There are people who went out of their way to crush us, and all were unsuccessful. In the same way, the Israelites took the Land of Canaan, promised to them by God. I guarantee these people the Israelites drove out had better-equipped, better-trained armies. They had the home-field advantage. Yet the Israelites annihilated them. The enemies were talented warriors, but the Israelites had God's giftedness on them and they overcame all odds.

Talents can be used selfishly; gifts are used to serve God's purposes. The clearest picture I can paint focuses on celebrities and some politicians. They may be worth hundreds of millions of dollars, but most of them use their wealth selfishly, living in mansions, collecting a fleet of cars, having servants to take care of their every needs, and living high-roller lifestyles. The fate of many is drug addiction, alcoholism, divorce, even suicide. They die miserable and before their time.

Had they been Christ-followers, they would have invested their wealth into Kingdom work. Charities that feed the poor and needy. Charities that evangelize and help people live life to the full. These investments pay back in big dividends and rewards both in the here and now and more importantly in the hereafter and throughout eternity.

> The outcome of a Spirit-filled life is unbelievable.
> And the gifts we're given are designed to uniquely fit our talents
> and then put them on steroids.

ᘓ♦ᘐ

So I have often wondered exactly what the "calling" is that we get for our lives from God Himself. Many people in the ministry say they are "called" to the ministry, but I have seen many "called" people who were in ministry and have made a complete mess of their lives.

Being called is finding your gifts and talents and then helping as many people in your profession as you can. One thing is certain: We are never called to do something we are not gifted at. In order to be effective in our efforts we need to study and educate ourselves to do our calling with purpose and do our jobs with excellence.

Several years ago, I had an occlusion in my left eye that caused blurriness and a real lack of vision in that eye. I was referred to a specialist who treats this condition. His diagnosis was that I would need to have eye injections every 7 to 8 weeks, probably for the rest of my life. My vision in this eye is still blurry, but I can see. He sees hundreds of patients, and he is the most caring professional I know. He told me that before this method of treatment was developed, all of his patients would now be blind in one or both eyes. He sees himself as a servant who is here to give sight to eyes that would otherwise be blind. That is what I consider a calling. I have told him his rewards will be many.

I was called to be in leadership and that brings with it many challenges and many opportunities as well. A good leader can be a culture warrior wherever he goes. Leaders with influence can change a bad culture into a good one. We can teach, we can serve, we can show kindness and become mentors. Character and leadership training is a calling in my life. One of my life goals is that people who have chosen to work for our company will not only make a good wage to support their families but will also have the tools for living a good life. Our leadership models and teaches these tools, so that our people can take the teaching and apply it in all of their lives.

Our past does not dictate what we can or cannot do. An example, again, is Paul in the Bible. He started out with a different name, Saul, and as a well-educated Jewish zealot. Anyone who defied his Jewish beliefs was considered fair game. Saul persecuted Christians, torturing and even killing them for their faith. Then he was stopped dead in his tracks by God. Blinded by the experience, he was told by God to go to the house of a Christian man, and this man would be able to restore his sight. This must have been humbling for Saul, because if he wanted help, he was being sent to a person he had been out to destroy. And this dude Saul had a really bad reputation among the Christians; he was a staunch enemy. But as a result of Saul's obedience, his eyes were opened, and he became a changed man with a new name and wrote much of the New Testament.

Paul's experience was a direct and dramatic calling, but for most of us our calling is a more subtle realization. So are people called to be business leaders, truck drivers, carpenters, or are these just our jobs? In Romans 12:7-8, Paul writes,

> If your gift is serving others, serve them well. If you are a teacher, teach well. If your gift is to encourage others, be encouraging. If God has given you leadership ability, take the responsibility seriously. And if you have a gift for showing kindness to others, do it gladly.

These gifts are broad in nature but can be used in most any job we work in.

Everyone can bring light to people who are in pain. Yesterday I had my knee replaced, and when I walked into the hospital in the morning, the first person I saw was my pastor, waiting for me to get there and to pray over me for a successful surgery. Another person who was carrying out his calling. The pre-op and post-op instructions and preparations were done by some wonderful, kind, and caring people who used their gifts and talents in a very good way. They were there for one reason, and that was to prepare for the surgery and do everything they could to make me comfortable. They made a difficult time for me much more pleasant. They prepped me for the surgery and made me feel comfortable. I had done the other knee several years ago and knew the process very well, but I dreaded the pain that was to follow. The doctor did a great job, and with the support of my walker, I walked out of the hospital in the afternoon after the morning surgery. Every person who attended to me was uniquely qualified to do their specific jobs, and the way they all cared for me was their calling. That is how our Creator wanted our culture to work—people helping people with competency, kindness, and caring for our fellow man.

Watch your thoughts,
for they become words.
Watch your words,
for they become actions.
Watch your actions,
for they become habits.
Watch your habits,
for they become character.
Watch your character,
for it becomes your destiny

—Lao Tzu

Chapter 7

The Bedrock of Our Culture

At the bottom of every building lies a structure that makes up the foundation of the building that sits on top of it. The lack of a rock-solid foundation is the sure demise of any building. So it is with our lives.

Without a firm foundation, our lives lack the stability it takes to run the race of life successfully. To finish well takes building on the bedrock of intentional values and principles. The Lodestar program identifies and defines 48 principles of character essential to building a strong foundation for the culture you long for and want to reproduce in your life. How well these character principles are learned and put into practice will be the real litmus test of who we are and how our life will impact those around us. These hallmarks of character are essential for living a God-honoring life. They will affect our marriages, our careers, and our relationships with others; and they will determine the level of success we achieve spiritually, physically, financially, and relationally.

I would suggest as you read through these principles in the appendix of this book, you jot down on each principle heading how you would rate yourself using a scale of 1 to 10. If there are any principles that you know you fall short of the midpoint of your grading (5 or less), I would encourage you to search for ways to bring that up to a grade of 7 to 10. Only one person in the history of our world has aced the test on every one of the principles. That man is Jesus Christ.

There are three steps to building this foundation and becoming culture warriors: Learn these character principles, live them, then teach them. Your family, business, church, and community will be stronger.

ഌ•ര

Of the 48 character principles, I would place *Forgiveness* in the #1 spot as essential for a strong foundation.

When forgiveness is not practiced, devastation ensues.

Unforgiveness will dump an enormous bucketful of vile and evil things into our lives that will stop all forward movement. An unforgiving heart can expect to suffer a long list of symptoms, some of which are anxiety, depression, insecurity, and fear. Over time, unforgiveness creates a hardened heart that squeezes out the love and happiness that is meant to soften our hearts. The health effects of unforgiveness can be seen in many hospital beds around the world. As some have said, unforgiveness is the poison we concocted for our enemy to drink; but we are daily sipping it ourselves, and it makes us sick, mentally, physically, and spiritually.

A friend gave me a copy of *Forgiveness... The Ultimate Miracle* by Paul J. Meyer. Meyer related this incredible story, as told to him by a friend:

> I visited a doctor in San Diego, California, several months ago. This doctor has treated over 15,000 terminally ill cancer patients. That's 15,000 individual cases! Almost all of them had been sent home to die by their own doctors, being given just months to live.
>
> They came to this doctor with the desperate hope that he might be able to help them. The record shows that 54 percent of his patients have lived more than five years, and

many have lived 10, 15, or more years. Some have died, but none of cancer.

I asked this doctor how he started a conversation with these patients, as many were depressed, some were angry at the world and at God, many were in great pain, and some were in wheelchairs, being too weak to walk. How do you start a conversation with such suffering, fear-ridden men, women, and children?

The doctor replied, "My first question is always the same—'Have you forgiven?'"

I was taken aback.

The doctor smiled. "The patients also give me a strange look and invariably ask, 'What does forgiveness have to do with my cancer?' I explain that we treat the complete individual. Man consists of body, soul, and spirit. If the soul or spirit is sick, then the body is bound to be sick also."

That made sense.

The doctor said, "I'll ask them, 'Have you forgiven the friend that cheated you? Have you forgiven your spouse? Your children? Your parents, who may not even be alive? Did you have trouble with your siblings because of inheritance quarrels? Have you forgiven them? Have you forgiven yourself for some stupidity in the past? Think back, have you forgiven?'"

He continued, "You are only hurting yourself, even destroying yourself, if you have not forgiven. You are not hurting the other person, who may even be dead. If you have not forgiven, you are locked up in a cage. This cage is filled with hate, resentments, and feelings of revenge. There is only one door out of this cage. There is a big sign on this door that says: Forgive. Open this door. Step out. Then you can breathe fresh air again, and a tremendous burden will fall from your shoulders."

The author of the book, Paul Meyer, adds:

> I find it extremely interesting that forgiveness is the first thing this doctor discusses with his terminally ill patients. If anyone questioned the power of forgiveness, there is no question anymore! Remember the doctor's results: 54 percent of his patients lived more than five years, many lived 10, 15, or more years. Some have died, but none of cancer!

If you or someone in your family is struggling with unforgiveness, I would advise you to get a copy of this tremendous book. You can find it on Amazon. I keep copies in my office to give to people who are hurting and have a hard time letting go of the past.

The Bible has much to say about forgiveness. In Romans 12:17-19 Paul writes,

> Repay no one evil for evil. Have regard for good things in the sight of all men. If it is possible, as much as lieth in you, live peaceably with all men. Beloved, do not avenge yourselves, but rather give place to wrath; for it is written, Vengeance is mine, I will repay, says the Lord. (KJV)

This is completely counterculture in today's society. Read the news or watch the local evening news. People kill other people out of anger, and revenge is the norm. Our prisons are full of unforgivers who have retaliated and killed or maimed someone who wronged them.

Most of us haven't gone to that extent, but we may be full of bitterness, which is "resentful cynicism that results in an intense antagonism or hostility towards others." The Bible teaches us to "get rid of all bitterness, rage, anger, harsh words, and slander, along with every form of malice." It then goes on to tell us how to deal with such bitterness and its fruits by being "kind and compassionate to one another, forgiving each other, just as in Christ God forgave you." (See Ephesians 4:31-32 NIV)

Another reason I picked this principle as a focus point is that almost everyone has struggled with forgiveness. In our society, lack of forgiveness is a culprit in all walks of life. It has divided this great country to the point where America is almost unrecognizable. It's not that our country's government has always been harmonious; many times parties are at odds with each other. It's the fact that today we have a media that fans the flames of vitriol and hatred. Almost everyone has access to this content, and feeding on it brainwashes a person. Many of the networks are based on lies and deceit. (Here is the real meaning of this deadly practice: "The action or practice of deceiving someone by concealing or misrepresenting the truth: a web of deceit/a series of lies and deceits.")

The mistake we make is hating the purveyors of this garbage. We need to remember the truth of the matter, given to us in Ephesians 6:12: "For we are not fighting against flesh-and-blood enemies, but against evil rulers and authorities of the unseen world, against mighty powers in this dark world, and against evil spirits in the heavenly places." People pushing this agenda are simply pawns in the hands of these dark powers, and most of them don't even know it. This is their foundation for spreading the bad culture. Their foundation is unsustainable, and it will all crumble in the end.

Let us not be disheartened by the direction our country and our world are heading. This world is not our home; we are only traveling through. Everything that is taking place has been foretold in the Bible, and we are the generation that's watching much of it come to pass. Our job is to be bold and courageous and step up our efforts to grow the culture of our homes, churches, and businesses by being vocal and getting involved in the fight. As believers, we are not called to be silent but to keep the lighthouse lit for all who need direction in navigating this dark world.

The reason we are not to let our hearts be troubled is simple: We know how the story is going to end. And that's the reason to stand on this cultural foundation. Nothing can shake us off and cause us to stray from what's right.

If you want to be fully informed about our future, turn off the television, turn off your phone and social media, and read these verses in either the New International Version or the New Living Translation: 2 Timothy 3:1-5; Matthew 24:36-44; 2 Peter 3:3-4; 1 Timothy 4:1; Luke 21:36; Mark 13:22; 2 Corinthians 11:13-15; Matthew 24:21-22; and all of the book of Revelation. It is so important for us to know the facts and to not be afraid. Everything that's happening is in God's plan. The prophecies are accurate and very relevant, even though they were written thousands of years ago. And God's plan is unfolding exactly the way God's Word says it will. Let us stand like a rock.

Question: When was the last time you heard a message or a series of messages in your church that enlightens us on the age we live in and uses this information as a call to arms on how to live in these times?

This principle of forgiveness is a culture maker in almost any setting—family, church, and the workplace. No matter who we are or how good our intentions, the fact is we are going to be hurt by others and others will be hurt by our words and actions as well. The antidote is not to simply gloss over wrongdoing by a family member, church member, or someone you work with. To simply forgive and not correct a wrong will in itself cause unforgiveness. Therefore, to keep the culture clean and healthy and maintain healthy relationships, we must confront and resolve wrongdoing.

The art of conflict resolution is not talked about as much as it should be because few people if any find it a pleasant task. Every mom, dad, husband, wife, employer, or employee will come face-to-face with this thorny issue—and few are well equipped to handle it. The majority of people will not face this head on so that they can move on, but instead will get bitter and angry and allow the relationship to die a slow, miserable death. This default behavior is one of the main reasons the divorce rate is over 50 percent in our country; and probably another 10 or 15 percent of couples have mediocre marriages and dysfunctional homes. The kids suffer the consequences and will repeat the same mistakes in their future homes. I lived this life in my childhood home. The culture was not good, and all of us who grew up there have struggled in our own lives as well.

ꕤ•ꕤ

Again, in our families and workplace, **the enemies of great culture are always at work trying to undermine what is good and wholesome**. It is the forces of evil that want to bring conflict and broken relationships into our lives.

It's not a question of whether or not we will have issues to deal with, we always will. Workplace conflict is a guaranteed fact, and so are family feuds. The question is, instead, how effectively and quickly we can spot the problems and get back on track. The bigger the company, the longer it usually takes for the CEO to find out about the problem and address it. When it comes to families, unresolved conflict is a surefire way to bring about bad culture. So the question is: How do we spot an issue before it is a three-alarm fire, and then how do we defuse it or settle it?

My training in dealing with conflict came from my experience growing up in a dysfunctional home. Dad was an authoritarian and was in a marriage that didn't work very well. He and Mom were extreme opposites and really never got on the same page. His work was his enjoyment, and us kids were for the most part an annoyance. Any conflict that persisted for any amount of time was dealt with by severe beatings. His handmade leather strap had been carefully crafted to inflict the ultimate pain.

Yes, I am all for disciplining children, and spanking as a last resort can be effective if not given in a fit of rage. Beatings, on the other hand, are never sanctioned in any family. When discipline turns violent and physically harmful, the battle is lost and the child will either stuff their resentment and anger down deep within their spirit or rebel and build up a deep hatred for the parents. I was in the latter camp. I knew the day was coming when the tables would be turned and I could inflict as much emotional pain on Dad as he did on me. When this home life was mixed with a religion that forced me to look and be someone I wasn't, it was a recipe for disaster.

The day of reckoning came when I was fourteen years old and strong and quick from working at jobs that required hard physical labor. Dad picked the wrong time to head for the drawer that was home to his leather strap. I stopped him and told him if he ever laid a hand on me again, I would beat him to a pulp. He looked at me with unbelief, and I asked him to step outside if he really wanted to give it a try. He never touched or threatened me again. And I took that carefully crafted, double-thick leather strap and cut it into little one-inch pieces so he could never use it again.

That was the day my life took a 90-degree turn. My dad no longer had the upper hand and couldn't lead me by intimidation and threats of punishment. In order to have any influence with me, he now had to talk to me as an adult; and for me to respond to his wishes, his tone of voice and demeanor needed to show respect for who I was and my opinions. One day, he looked at me in frustration and asked why I couldn't respond like his friend's boys did to their father. I answered his question with a question; I asked him why he couldn't treat me the way his friend treated his boys. Point made! Later on in life, I realized that at that point in our relationship, he actually respected me for standing my ground against his irrational rants. I was a fighter and not a pushover, and to him, that showed I was a potential leader. That was the reason he chose me to be his successor in his future business.

About four years later when I met the girl I would eventually marry, I saw in her outstanding family how a good-culture family unit looked and functioned. It wasn't perfect, but the stability and culture came first and foremost from a husband and wife who loved each other dearly and were in synch with their values, and the children followed their parents' example. I realized that a cohesive family was a true gift of God, and I wanted that more than anything else in life.

My childhood was ruined because of unresolved conflict between my mom and my dad. That is why conflict left unchecked is such a deadly weapon of destruction in our culture. It is the poison that kills homes, relationships, and our workplaces. Most importantly, it skews the way we see our Heavenly Father. A young, impressionable child will soon decide that if the Heavenly Father is anything like their earthly father, then thank you, but no thank you.

I married a great and godly woman. I accepted Jesus Christ as my personal Lord and Savior. I read hundreds of books. And somewhere I came to the realization that God is a God of love who can and will be our savior. I know my eternal future is secure with Him. And I am free of the bondage I grew up in.

And by the way, when I mentioned the word *religion* earlier, I came to realize that religion does not signify a person is a Christ follower. As a matter of fact, the religious leaders of Jesus' day were the very ones who plotted and asked the authorities to execute Him for His teachings.

It's a messed-up world we live in, and today's view of one Lord, one Savior, and one set of teachings to follow is being challenged and turned away from at a faster and faster pace. Also rejected is the real truth about sin. Our society has changed the definition of sin and has said we have a right to live however we want to. This is the real reason the cultures of our country, our homes, and our workplaces are in decline—one simple three-letter word: SIN. The only antidote for this terrible disease is found in the Bible, the author being Jesus Christ.

How then can we bring this doctrine into our workplace and our homes and set up a great culture in a sin-filled world?

ꕥ♦ꕥ

In the workplace, we have a large diversity of people coming from all kinds of homes and life experiences. With an average of 350 people now at Weaver Leather, our employees' backgrounds and beliefs ranged from Amish and Mennonite to completely unchurched folks.

Once a month for over 25 years, I taught the Lodestar Guidance character principles to institute the culture I wanted, because having a great culture really comes down to having and living lives of good character.

Even though every one of these principles is found and taught in the Bible, the acceptance and buy-in on this program has been excellent. Not because everyone was a born-again Christ follower, but because they saw and experienced our culture and loved what it does to a workplace. We were never heavy-handed with the spiritual content, but we also did not shy away from it.

Over the years, these meetings helped us develop a culture that I am very proud of. When people left our company to either get married or change jobs, we asked them to fill out an exit-interview form with a variety of questions asking how we could have served them better. There's also a question about what they most enjoyed about their employment with our company. Many of these people picked our Lodestar Guidance program as the thing they enjoyed the most and that most benefitted them. They said it not only helped them at their job, but made a big difference in their homes and personal lives as well. Many companies are now using this platform, and the information to obtain the program is all in the Appendix of this book.

Great culture is always intentional; it is never just a natural occurrence. It is up to you, the owner, leader, or parent to make the decision on how serious you are about creating this type of culture which brings rewards in ways unimaginable.

The rewards I am talking about are both tangible and intangible. The cost of implementing this is not in dollars. It will cost you, but it will be your sacrifice of time and in vulnerability while teaching principles that you yourself might lack. Not only will most of your people already know that you lack some of those principles, but they will also expect you to acknowledge it. That's when real growth happens and you become a better leader while your employees learn from your example.

My legacy will not be packaged in the size or profitability of the companies I've been involved with over my lifetime, but it will be in the culture I helped to put in place, a culture that propelled us forward and made us industry leaders. And, more importantly, it is a culture that has had an impact on the lives of those who chose to spend the best years of their lives with us.

A culture of accountability makes a good organization great and a great organization unstoppable.

—Henry Evans

Chapter 8

Accountability

On January 28, 1986, the space shuttle *Challenger* launched from the Kennedy Space Center in Florida. In less than two minutes, it exploded, killing all seven on board.

The day before the launch, Bob Ebeling and four other engineers who had worked on the booster rocket were engaged in a desperate attempt to stop the launch. They spoke with their boss, who was their company's representative with NASA. They tried to convince NASA officials and their own engineering company that the launch should be delayed because of the cold overnight temperatures. The engineers worried that the cold could cause rubber O-ring seals on the shuttle to fail. "We all knew that if the seals failed, the shuttle would blow up," Ebeling said in an interview with NPR.[1]

Politics and agenda overruled, and because these engineers were not heard (although they spent hours presenting data that showed the danger), NASA went ahead with the launch. The consequences were deadly. Along with others, Ebeling wept as he saw the Challenger explode.

---

[1] https://www.npr.org/sections/thetwo-way/2016/03/21/470870426/challenger-engineer-who-warned-of-shuttle-disaster-dies accessed 4/5/2023.

Weeks after, he and one other engineer told their story about attempting to stop the launch. But they did it anonymously, fearing they would lose their jobs with the engineering company who had sided with NASA and okayed the launch. Thirty years later, after a lifetime of being haunted by his own ineffectiveness in stopping the launch, Ebeling was not afraid to be identified when NPR interviewed him. "Somebody should tell... the truth," he said.

That's how deadly it can be when a company, an organization, or an individual is not held accountable to the truth. NASA eventually did make the statement that the tragic deaths served as a reminder to the space agency "to remain vigilant and to listen to those like Mr. Ebeling who have the courage to speak up."[2]

Most decisions are not this drastic, but over time, the erosion of trust and accountability lead to heartbreaking outcomes. Infractions may start small, but they will grow into ever bigger abuses with more damaging results if accountability is not embraced.

It's much easier to decide what our core values are and what we want our culture to be than to hold ourselves and others accountable. But without accountability, our mission statement is not worth the paper it was written on. I have seen plenty of companies that look nothing like the fancy documents they have put together. As important as it is to set up a plan for how we live life together as a family or how we work together as a business, the tough part is enforcing it, with no exceptions.

The lack of accountability has become a customary part of our society's culture. Very few people would say that they enjoy confrontations and conflict. (If they do enjoy these two principles, they might just be jerks who are always spoiling for a good fight.)

---

[2] https://www.npr.org/sections/thetwo-way/2016/03/21/470870426/challenger-engineer-who-warned-of-shuttle-disaster-dies accessed April 5, 2023

We simply hide our true feelings and pretend all is well and stuff our anger and resentment down into our very being. In the long run, this produces bitterness, anger, and unforgiveness.

The most often used excuse for people failing to lovingly confront people of evil is the age-old pretext that "we love them so much and don't want to hurt their feelings." That is not the real truth. The real truth is that we ourselves are afraid of being hurt if conflict ensues or being rejected or shunned by the other person. If our motives are right in holding someone accountable, we have done our God-given job, whether it's taken well or not. Our motivation should be God-centered; if it is, long-term good will usually come from this. Really, if we see no good result immediately, so be it. Jesus, our perfect example, was very direct with His accusers, and His words cut them to their hearts—to the point that they conspired in plots to kill Him. And in the end, they succeeded.

So the question is, **are we willing to confront evil in our day by speaking truth?** There is a price to pay, but that shouldn't stop us from firmly rebuking sin and evil. No matter what we set up as our rules and standards for the culture we want and expect, the chances are 100 percent that people will challenge and step across the line and that conflict will ensue. There are always people who will challenge what we have set up as our standard.

Lack of accountability wreaks havoc on the culture in the family. If the curfew for your teenager is 12:00 and he or she sneaks in at 2:00 a.m. and nothing really happens about the infraction, you just lost control and your other standards will get blown off as well.

Maintain accountability, and in doing so, follow my uncle Ervin's wise model. He and his wife were not able to have children, but he told me it seemed fairly easy, in his mind, as to how the family unit should function. He said he always envisioned setting up guidelines for kids up to the age when they moved out of the house. These "rules" would set the guardrails as wide as possible, but when someone was found on the other side of them, that person would be brought to accountability quickly and consistently.

For families, many conflicts result from setting little nitpicky rules that are meaningless. That's what caused 80 percent of the conflict in our home as I was growing up. The way I cut my hair, the clothes I wore—there were literally dozens of dos and don'ts that didn't amount to 5 cents. Thomas Jefferson gave wise advice when he said, "In matters of style, swim with the current. In matters of principle, stand like a rock." Following this principle alone would have saved our family from many needless fights when words were spoken in the heat of the argument that damaged relationships.

We should always be tactful and try not to offend the other person, but there is a time and a place when we need to speak the truth even if it's not the popular thing to do. Leviticus 19:17 says this: "Do not nurse hatred in your heart for any of your relatives. Confront people directly so you will not be held guilty for their sin." That's pretty clear that failing to rebuke and confront them when we see them living in sin is the equivalent of not loving them enough to share the truth. In Romans 1:28, Paul wrote, "Since they thought it foolish to acknowledge God, he abandoned them to their foolish thinking and let them do things that should never be done." When we abandon someone, it means they are free to choose the road to destruction, and we won't even try to stop them or warn them. Hebrews 12:6 gives us the opposite: "For the Lord disciplines those he loves, and he punishes each one he accepts as his child."

Charlie Munger, influential leader of Berkshire Hathaway, gave a graduation speech at Harvard in 1986.[3] His topic was

[3] https://jamesclear.com/great-speeches/how-to-guarantee-a-life-of-misery-by-charlie-munger accessed April 5, 2023

"How to Guarantee a Life of Misery." I would dare say that no one in their right mind would want to be miserable, but he used this recipe for a miserable life to highlight the opposite—principles for a productive and un-miserable life. One of these principles, expressed in the negative, was "Be Unreliable."

> "[If you want to guarantee a life of misery], be unreliable. Do not faithfully do what you have engaged to do. If you will only master this one habit, you will more than counterbalance the combined effect of all your virtues, howsoever great. If you like being distrusted and excluded from the best human contribution and company, this prescription is for you. Master this one habit and you can always play the role of the hare in the fable, except that instead of being outrun by one fine turtle you will be outrun by hordes and hordes of mediocre turtles and even by some mediocre turtles on crutches.
>
> I must warn you that if you [do the opposite] it may be hard to end up miserable, even if you start disadvantaged. I had a roommate in college who was and is severely dyslexic. But he is perhaps the most reliable man I have ever known. He has had a wonderful life so far, outstanding wife and children, chief executive of a multibillion dollar-corporation... You simply can't count on your other handicaps to hold you back if you persist in being reliable."

Munger's prescription for misery includes being completely unreliable, having no accountability to anyone.

Reading this speech brought a smile to my face but reality to my thinking. Some years ago, I was introduced to a speaker by the name of Mike Scott. His message and program are called "Totally Accountable Systems." Without a doubt, this was the most comprehensive study on the topic I have ever been through.

If your business is looking for a speaker whose programs will bring great results, this is your man.

The principle of accountability covers the entire scope of our lives. From family to church to business, from the little things to the very important issues, accountability is key to the culture we want.

ഇ•ര

During my 40-year tenure at Weaver Leather, countless infractions came up that were counter to the culture we held dear. There is no time like the present to take care of these problems. Everyone—and I do mean everyone—is watching to see what will happen when the culture is challenged. First the manager is scrutinized. People lose confidence in weak managers, and as time passes by, the boss will also lose the confidence of his people when his appointed leaders fail and the boss either doesn't know or doesn't care about it.

That's why management by "walking around" is so important. We can't stay hidden in our office or bury ourselves in countless meetings to the point we don't have time to talk and mingle with the people doing the jobs on the floor, in the warehouse, in the customer service department, and in every other facet of our business. When we're out and about and available to our people, the real influencers who care about our culture will let us know where the hotspots are. We need to keep our finger on the pulse of the company and keep the culture free from anyone who wants to sabotage it.

The larger the company, the more we need vice presidents, COOs, HR managers, and parallel positions staffed with people who are culture warriors. It's critical to use the chain of command and insist that managers do the job of correcting people because as the company grows, the president and CEO can't possibly catch and address all poor character. We must empower our leadership team to handle these confrontations in a structured and timely manner.

As leaders and culture warriors, we can build accountability in these ways:

1) Be thorough and extremely detailed on what you expect, leaving nothing to chance. Tell your team what the job entails: time lines, check points, and finish date and time.

2) Be sure to include the why. It's important for people to understand the full meaning of why we are going to do whatever we are planning to do.

3) Ask for feedback, questions, and even pushback on why this is so important. The time to dissent on doing the project is before we hit the Go button.

4) Ask the group to repeat back to you what you have communicated to them, so there is absolute clarity.

5) The final step is to ask for an "I am all in" statement.

6) Then offer help if anyone gets stuck or bogged down on the project. Silence is not golden, and to let an issue ride and not ask for help until the deadline is being non-accountable.

7) Encourage the team to stay connected during the process and to hold each other accountable as well.

8) Celebrate the success and give credit where credit is due.

I have found that during this process, people will come to you, the CEO or boss, with a problem they have encountered and will usually bypass their manager if possible. This is not because they think you, the boss, are so smart; they do this because it's the best way to pass the buck: "The boss told me to do it this way." If they've bypassed their manager, ask them to go back and touch base. Note: It's good to check back with their manager and see if they did as you asked.

Even if they do check with their manager before they come to you, never let them leave your office with the monkey on your back instead of on theirs. Help them out, give them direction, but make sure the monkey stays on their back. Often, I would direct an employee to make a phone call to someone I knew but they didn't. The minute the forward motion of the project rests on your shoulders to make the next move, they have successfully unloaded the monkey onto your back. If there is an exception to this rule and you bring them the information they need, let them know that they own their part of the project in full again.

ᘓ•ᘏ

Of all the problems that face a boss, the worst is the customer who agreed to the terms of sale and then simply didn't follow those terms. At one point, Weaver Leather went with terms of 2 percent discount if paid in 10 days and net 30 days. That turned out to be a really bad idea. Customers paid in 30 days and took the 2 percent discount. To post that unpaid 2 percent to their account as a receivable infuriated the customer. So we eliminated the 2 percent discount because the vast majority of customers would cheat on the 10-day requirement. Customers who did not follow the terms of sale went on C.O.D., and they had to pay the delivery person. The credit card era ended that.

But hard-pay customers still persisted, and they nearly always used the same tactics: 1) They rarely if ever called in and asked for extra time to pay because of a difficulty they were experiencing. 2) They wouldn't respond to reminders and overdue statements. 3) They couldn't be reached by phone. To add insult to injury, they would often place big orders with urgent deadlines. Nearly all of these customers are no longer in business.

That's why character in business is so very important. If we don't pay our vendors on time, every time, why would we be surprised when our customers don't pay us on time? The law of sowing and reaping holds true. The harvest of what you sow may not show up on your doorstep the next morning, but know this—that law is 100 percent certain.

ꕥ

Nowhere in our society is the lack of accountability more flagrant than in our federal government. When you watch the sound bites of what politicians promised during their campaign days and measure their actions now against those promises, they are often doing the opposite of what they said they'd do.

Who holds them accountable? If they are Democrats, the media will many times cover for them. It should be we the people, but many people will vote along party lines and continue to elect the same candidates if their party has given voters enough free stuff.

John Emerich Edward Dalberg Acton was an English politician and historian. Known as Lord Acton, he wrote in 1887, "Power tends to corrupt and absolute power corrupts absolutely. Great men are almost always bad men." This is nothing new to society. Today, many have sold their souls to the almighty dollar. Their salaries do not represent their net worth, and they are paid by those who need their blessing. This practice reaches all the way to the top, and it is found in both parties of the government. 1 Timothy 6:10 says "For the love of money is the root of all kinds of evil. And some people, craving money, have wandered from the true faith and pierced themselves with many sorrows."

Blindfolded Lady Justice we see on our courthouse holding the scales of justice has had her blindfold removed and injustice is now the norm. As a result, our country is divided as it was during the Civil War. If our enemies are patient, there will be no need to fire missiles to take our republic down. We have met the enemy, and it is us.

ꟷ♦ꟷ

As people of faith, we tend to be quiet when evil rears its ugly head. We do this in the name of humility—which in reality is cowardice. To disagree and hold people accountable by speaking truth is a matter of courage and conviction.

To call people out when they are wreaking havoc on our culture is our job, and when we do it in the right way, it can be effective. Two of the best books I have read on this subject are national best sellers, *Crucial Confrontations* and *Crucial Conversations.* I read and reread these books and learned that there really is a good way to disagree and to hold people accountable without destroying the relationship.

My takeaway on having crucial confrontations was to: Gather all the facts available, then talk one on one with the person. Address the issue and explain how this is not what was agreed upon or what is morally right. Then let the other person give their version of the issue for which they've been called on the carpet. Give them a chance to gracefully confess and come clean. If they don't, state the facts that you have learned and ask them to do a course correction. Explain the consequences should this behavior continue, and encourage them to think about how this could impact their future. Follow up a week later and see if there is progress being made. If no changes are forthcoming, ask them to leave your organization. This is obviously a much-abbreviated explanation of the process laid out in the book. It's an excellent framework for holding others in our workplace accountable.

These guidelines are important even outside the workplace. Every day we meet and interact with people we disagree with; we can let them know we disagree and let them know *why* we disagree, and then just ask them to think about our conversation. Jesus did this so very well. He never condoned sin or accepted a lifestyle that was wrong, but he explained the wrong and its consequences and asked a person to repent and follow his teachings. Today he would be condemned as a "hater" for not condoning and accepting sin.

Having the courage to stand up for what's right and push back on evil is a must if we are to see real and meaningful change in this country. Teach the truth at home. Teach the truth at work. Live a life that matches what you teach. That's my definition of a culture warrior. It may seem that we are outnumbered, but in actuality, we are usually not. We are simply a silent majority giving way to the vocal minority. And even if we are the minority, when we do our part and ask God to do the rest, we automatically become the majority.

Even though this is the least enjoyable part of leadership, think of it as the pressure cooker that preserves products we put into it, protecting them from spoiling for years to come. Everyone benefits from accountability. It builds trust and offers confidence that someone really cares about the wellness of our families, our workplace, or our social groups. The key is always to speak the truth in love. It never fails in the long run. And if you hold yourself accountable as well, the person who benefits the most will be you.

The Bible clearly calls for accountability, and, ultimately, every person will be held accountable to God:

"As surely as I live," says the LORD, 'every knee will bend to me, and every tongue will declare allegiance to God."Yes, each of us will give a personal account to God. Romans 14:11-12

A cheerful heart is good medicine, but a broken spirit saps a person's strength.

—Proverbs 17:22

Chapter 9

The Fun Factor

Happy ties that make lasting memories are an important part of good culture. For family, it's times spent together enjoying each other's company, special times like trips taken together or simple, ordinary moments that cause us to laugh just remembering...

These are memories I don't have from my growing up years. That doesn't mean I have to repeat the pattern in my family, and it doesn't mean I live my life in resentment of an unhappy childhood. Forgive and move on. Yes, the scars remain, but they don't dictate my life. I loved my father and mother, and I plan to see them in heaven sometime.

Families that do have a great culture experience a strong bond between siblings, even after the parents are no longer here. I see that in my wife's family. Good times and good memories in their formative years have given way to good times with their family in later years.

But in our larger society, good culture in families seems to be deteriorating. With a divorce rate of over 50 percent in our country, many families are estranged from each other and the family circle is broken.

The cause is that our culture is no longer based on Judeo-Christian principles, and the secular movement cannot and will not embrace these values. Don't get me wrong, I know there are still millions of great-culture Christ followers in our country, but the trend is going in the wrong direction. The evil one is very busy destroying families, because he knows as the family goes, so goes the culture of our republic.

A happy home can replicate itself for generations to come. An unhappy home can also produce unhappy homes for generations to come. Unless someone breaks the unhealthy cycle, it will continue. Our pastor, Dwight Mason, has said many times that the best gift we can give our children is for them to see the love and tenderness shared between their parents. Even though I didn't see that growing up, our kids did get to see their mom and dad love and cherish each other.

So what's the secret in getting our families back on track? It's this simple; **It's a matter of choices and decisions we make early on**. Out of the thousands of decisions we will make in our life time, two choices will have the most indelible effect on our lives. One is our decision about our faith, and the other is the choice of a husband or wife. These two life-altering decisions play a heavy part in determining how the culture will look in our homes and our lives in general.

Our faith will prompt us to make choices that keep us healthy and growing; at the same time, it keeps us from doing things that will harm us in the future. Our choice of life partner will largely determine if your home will be a happy place to raise your kids or if they will see a dysfunctional home. In either instance, it also will affect their future families.

ഇ•ഗ

A happy workforce is more highly motivated, more capable of producing at higher levels, more attractive to potential hires, and more tightly knit. Face it, people want to work with people they like and have fun with. All of that makes it very difficult for someone else to poach one of our good people.

At work, the culture is shaped quite differently than in a family. Many people converge at the workplace, and they all come with different personalities and experiences in families with different cultures. At times, creating the culture you desire with so many differences in people may seem like herding cats, but the real key to infusing the culture with the values we want is often making the workplace fun.

That's easier said than done, but the first step toward creating a lively and happy culture is for us as owners and/or CEOs to get out on the floor on a regular basis and spread some sunshine. Time spent with our people both in the offices and on the floor is time well spent. It's a great stress reliever, both for you and your team.

One of the keys to being a fun boss to work for is to focus not on yourself and your pressing problems but to focus on your people. You may think you are the most important factor that drives your company forward, but after all, without your people, you'll have no company. They are the lifeblood of any organization, and you are there to produce a great culture and to make each one of your people successful.

The top dog needs to be a likeable person; that's one of our Lodestar principles. People respond very well to the likeable person but are turned off by the serious, all-business, somber, and frowny-type person who stays in his office. Leadership plays a large part in infusing the fun factor in a culture. Whenever people tiptoe around an unhappy leader, the effects are always negative.

So let's look at the meaning of *likeability*. It is simply being agreeable and approachable. Here's a snapshot of what a likeable person would look like: They are pleasant, and others are attracted by their sympathy and empathy. They are endearing, genial, and engaging. At the opposite end of the spectrum is the person who is not likeable: disagreeable, harsh, and uncaring. They are usually difficult to please, irritable, and unapproachable. Which of these two we really are will be reflected in the culture of our company.

You might say, "I am an introvert and I don't enjoy interacting with people. I like to keep to myself." Well, that excuse just doesn't fly with me, because I am an introvert. But I can be as engaging and humorous as anyone. I just can't do it for ten hours a day every day. After a busy and hectic day, I wind down by going on a long, quiet walk with my yellow Lab, Sam. He understands me and loves to be with me no matter how solemn or happy I am. In other words, I need to recharge my batteries.

In Chapter 4, we talked about the cultural leader and the personal qualities needed to be successful. If we were to create an accurate profile of 100 executives or managers, their personalities would be all across the board. Some are outgoing and fun to work with; some are dead serious and have the weight of the world on their shoulders and have little to say. I don't have any sympathy for the overworked, tired, and cranky boss. Here's why: Each of us has a choice in what we delegate and to whom we delegate. Delegation is a critical part of leadership. If, as the boss, we think we can do most things better than our staff and we'll have to do it ourselves if we want it done right, then our future will not be pretty. We'll lose great talent because our team members couldn't spread their wings and grow. We'll lose "10s" and have to hire "5s." In the end, we'll be old and broken down at a young age.

One of my favorite authors, Dale Carnegie, has summed this up well: "People rarely succeed unless they have fun in what they are doing." So I would encourage everyone to do a "fun check" in your jobs. If you're not having fun and it's a result of your job, first take a real close look at the person in the mirror, because chances are good that your unhappiness is caused by that person.

If the culture at your workplace is toxic and you're the leader, FIX IT. If you can't change the culture because you're not in a position to do so, by all means, leave! Because as Carnegie said, you won't succeed if you're not having fun at what you're doing.

༄•༄

Company picnics, Christmas banquets, and other social gatherings with our workforce is a great way of having fun and showing appreciation, but nothing beats one-on-one time with our team members. Over the past several years, a few friends and I built a sporting clays course. It's a great way to spend time with the people who have chosen a career at your place of business. It's been inspirational to watch company groups get together and enjoy a round of competitive clay shooting. As a matter of fact, if you're ever in the area, give us a call and we will set you up with whatever you need to enjoy a round of shooting those elusive clay targets. Google airportridgesportingclays.com and call 330-674-2777. You can even fly your plane in, and we will pick you up.

For people who embrace the idea of spending time with their associates doing something fun, activities like this are time and money well spent. When we go from boss-and-employee to a true friendship, relationships go to a much higher level. The idea that business relationships and personal friendships should be kept separate doesn't fly with me. Some of my dearest friends are people who spent the best years of their lives with our company. I owe them more than they owe me. These great people could have had jobs with many different companies, but they chose to give me the best they had to give, and I will be forever grateful for their service and loyalty to myself and the company.

It seems that every department in our company has someone who keeps things lively and fun. Over the years, we had many of these people, and I call them "spark plugs." They ignite the fun factor and always seem to have an encouraging word or humor that keeps morale high. These people are true influencers. They get the best results without coercion. They don't have to force or browbeat people to do their best. They can be funny and usually have a good story to tell others. One of these people was my brother David. He had a sense of humor and could turn almost anything into a laughing matter. When he went on vacation, people complained that work was boring.

There were countless others who brought the fun factor into our culture. Myron, Dad's first employee, is still with us, and his energy and lively conversation are contagious. He worked fast and laughed often. Often, when an applicant was looking for a job, Myron would take them on a quick tour of our workplace. We had a long ramp that led from our assembly building to our warehouse. Myron was always at full speed, and when he got to the top of the ramp, he would look back to see how far the applicant was behind him. If it was more than four or five steps, Myron was concerned that this person couldn't keep up with his pace and may not be a good candidate. Even in his sixties, he can still outpace and outwork people half his age. He has a heart of gold, and without his leadership and git-er-done work ethic, our company wouldn't be where it is today.

Nowhere is it more important to have a happy workplace than our Customer Service department. My theory has always been, Happy workers, happy customers. These girls answer thousands of phone calls in a day's time, and no matter how professional they are, it is their demeanor that resonates with the caller, both for the good and the bad. In the close quarters and the small cubicles of this department, it only takes one sourpuss to put a wet blanket on the entire group. Then it's better to put that one person in a corner where they can't infect others around them with their bad attitude. Or… don't have them around at all.

Since my retirement, I don't see these people very often; but when I do drop by, it's still great people and great culture. Weaver Leather hires many younger people, many of whom are teenagers. Having a fun and happy culture is so very important in hiring and retaining these young people. The norm for young Amish girls is to leave once they get married, but then, having them recommend our company as a great place to work is priceless.

℘•ↄ

If you're looking for ways to put some fun back into your family or your workforce, try incorporating more of these three things to lighten the spirit of your culture.

1. Humor. I love to be around people who make me laugh. The power of a simple smile is amazing, and a good joke can change my day. It's a big deal when the boss stops by and has no agenda except to converse with a team member. Save up some good stories that will make people laugh.

The old saying is that laughter is the best medicine, and it's true. The benefits of laughter are many. Laughter triggers healthy physical and emotional changes in the body and has some real health benefits. It can strengthen our immune system, boost our mood, and diminish pain. It also protects us from dangerous and damaging stress. Nothing has more power to bring your mind and body back into balance than a good laugh. Humor lightens your burdens, inspires hope, and keeps us grounded and focused and alert. A good laugh can even bring tears to your eyes that will relieve tension and stress and leave your muscles relaxed for long periods of time. Laughter connects us to others and helps us to release anger and forgive sooner. But remember, getting a good laugh about the stupid things that we have done is okay when we laugh at ourselves. But having a good laugh at the expense of someone else is highly risky.

2. Encouragement. Mark Twain said, "I can live for two months on a good compliment." A second characteristic of a fun and happy culture is lots of encouraging words. A compliment from the boss or your spouse goes a long way. Why? Because in our toxic world culture today, not many encouraging words and compliments are found.

I seldom—maybe never—received compliments from my dad. That is, until the day he passed away in the blink of an eye. The day after Thanksgiving, our business was closed, but we were working together taking inventory of our leather. Dad gave me a couple of compliments that day that shocked me, and after 31 years of hearing no compliments, I started to think that he might have taken to drinking. The fact that I am writing about this day and what an impact his words had on me and still have 38 years later, is a prime example on how long a sincere compliment can have meaning. He died that evening. How timely were his words of encouragement and advice that day! Those words gave me the confidence to take our company from its infancy to over 300 people in the next 40 years.

We never know how a well-placed compliment can encourage people to do things they never thought possible. So find someone doing something right, better than average, and let them know that you noticed and you appreciate their best efforts. And if you're the recipient of a compliment, you might say, "Thank you! You made my day" or "I thought about what you said, and I thank you for noticing."

3. Goodness. Dennis Prager wrote, "Goodness is about character - integrity, honesty, kindness, generosity, moral courage, and the like. More than anything else, it is about how we treat other people." I really think this personifies who we should be, not only in our workplace and home but in interactions with everyone we meet. This lines up with Jesus' teaching and His actions. He had all the power in Heaven and Earth, but He associated with people of all classes and situations in life. He treated them with *goodness.* He is our perfect example.

The principle of fun and happiness is well worth our time to teach and practice in our home and our workplace. It's another arrow in the quiver of the great-culture warrior.

To everything there is a season,
a time for every activity under heaven.
A time to be born and a time to die.
A time to plant and a time to harvest.
A time to kill and a time to heal.
A time to tear down and a time to build up.
A time to cry and a time to laugh.
A time to grieve and a time to dance.
A time to scatter stones and a time to gather stones.
A time to embrace and a time to turn away.
A time to search and a time to quit searching.
A time to keep and a time to throw away.
A time to tear and a time to mend.
A time to be quiet and a time to speak.
A time to love and a time to hate.
A time for war and a time for peace.

—Solomon, Ecclesiastes 3:1-8

Chapter 10

The 4 Seasons of Our Lives

The seasons of the year also define our seasons in life. Fresh and new springtime personifies our childhood years. Vibrant summer is the equivalent of the strong and energetic prime of our youth, after which comes the autumn of middle-age. And then winter settles in as we move into our senior years.

In **the springtime** of life, core values are formed, grow, and mature. The culture children grow up in has profound and long-term effects on the remaining three seasons of life.

The ideal scenario is that a child grows up (let's say from ages 0 to 12) with their mother and father in a loving and nurturing home, where they learn from a very young age the core values that Mom and Dad teach and live. The culture is warm, accepting, loving, and happy. There are boundaries, and done right, these boundaries become a part of the child's security. Ideally, the parents are Christians and use biblical principles to live and to parent. The child is taken to church on a regular basis and is learning that the Bible is the guide for living.

I am well aware that today's modern education says we should not force our religious beliefs on our children. Here is the irrationality of such a statement: No one can *force* anyone to believe anything. Even God allows us to choose our own path. Proverbs 22:6 says, "Train up a child in the way he should go, and when he is old, he will not depart from it." If we don't teach and train our children, someone else will, and that someone may be totally off base but our child will buy into his way of thinking.

School is a part of the maturing stage. Mom and Dad aren't there, and children are exposed to others from varying cultures, some good and some not so good. They can see for themselves how other children behave, and they will soon understand that not every home is a safe place for the kids. By age 8 or 9, a child has already developed their own characteristic ways of seeing life. They are also discovering some of their own interests. The bookworm, for example, wants to read and study, is fascinated by information, and wants to learn all there is about life and how it is lived.

At that age, I loved to read books about people who lived life outdoors in remote wilderness settings. I read every Danny Orlis book in the series, and my love of hunting, fishing, hiking, and exploring was firmly ingrained by the time I was 8, maybe even before. The contention I saw in our family made me angry, and my escape was the great outdoors with my dog Biff. I am now in the winter season of life, and guess what? My favorite part of the day is to take my faithful Lab, Sam, and walk the hills and woods of our farm. Even though in my youth the outdoors was an escape from the bad culture of home and now our marriage is solid and blissful, I still unwind with nature and my buddy Sam. By the way, Sam is also in the winter years of his life, and he has aches and pains just like I do. That's okay. I have slowed my pace and so has he.

School was a necessary evil for me but I managed to have a C average throughout my school years. My future was being shaped by school, my friends, and my family. *Love* was only a word we read about in the Bible, and I was confused because my heavenly Father was said to be the essence of love and caring, but my earthly father was unhappy, angry, and very strict. If my heavenly Father was actually like my earthly father, why would I want to follow Him? Fortunately, I later figured out two things: Dad wasn't the bad guy I thought he was, and we cannot compare God to an earthly father.

The spring season of life is so very important. Little minds are like sponges, and everything seen and heard leaves a big impression that the thirsty sponge soaks up, both for the good and the bad. Gladys and I have precious grandsons, and it is a great thrill to see them starting life in a successful way, growing, developing, accepting Christ as their Savior, and being baptized.

For children in a bad-culture home, the springtime of life is a very different experience. Today the US has the world's highest rate of children living in single-parent homes—nearly 24 million children, 80 percent of whom live with mother only. The effects are not at all healthy. They face the risk of emotional and behavioral challenges like aggression and high-risk behaviors. If you turn on the evening news, you will see young teenagers hijacking cars or shooting people with no remorse or conscience whatsoever. This is one big reason why we have the crisis of crime on our streets today. Unless someone intervenes or something drastic happens, these young minds will act out whatever was allowed to enter in. These young people are headed for a tragic life. Our culture as a country is entrapped in this trend, and it is progressively intensifying. Many youngsters die on the streets, are in prison, or belong to a drug gang.

Those in our government can't even manage themselves, so we need not look for a solution forthcoming from them. This culture is a direct result of our country turning its back on Judeo-Christian values; when those values are abandoned, evil has full rein. **We don't have a crime problem in our country; we have a spiritual problem.**

ᘓ•ᘎ

As youth enter the workplace or get an education for a career, life can become challenging. In **the summer season,** young adults face many potential obstacles with jobs, choosing spouses, and making some important decisions at this time of life. The good part of this summer season is that minds and bodies are fully developed, and young adults have incredible energy and capacity to undertake even the most demanding jobs. The danger in this season is that many lack maturity and then it's easy to make unwise choices that will negatively affect the future. Core values may or may not have been fully established at the onset of summer, and so the culture a young person settles into can lead them down the wrong road. This is where an ounce of prevention is worth a pound of cure.

During this season, a good, qualified mentor will put one on a good pathway. I've had good mentors in my life, and they kept me from doing some really stupid things. Bobb Biehl authored a book on mentoring[4] and is an authority on the subject. I have had the honor of meeting with him and getting some very wise council. His definition for mentoring is: "Making available the mentor's personal strength, resources, and network (friendships/contacts) to help the protégé reach his or her goals." The benefits of using a mentor are countless.

Choosing a good, qualified mentor is the important first step. Here are just a few guidelines from Bobb's book:

A. Your mentor should always be the same sex as you are.

---

[4] from Mentoring: Confidence in Finding a Mentor and Becoming One, Bobb Biehl, B&H Pub Group, January 1, 1997, material used with permission.

B. Parents and siblings normally don't work out too well as mentors. Parents have a great deal of influence, but mentoring is a different type of relationship, where you have someone you can tell your darkest secrets and feel safe doing it.
C. Pick someone older and more experienced than you in business and life in general.
D. Make sure the person you ask shares the values you hold dear or that you admire.
E. Don't be afraid to ask someone to meet with you. Most people are flattered by being asked to mentor someone. Often, while the protégé is wondering, *Why would this outstanding person want to help me?* the mentor might be wondering, *Do I have anything to teach this exceptionally gifted person?*

Everybody has their own share of baggage. So does your mentor. He or she is not perfect, and that's part of the value they can bring to you. Letting you know their mistakes will be a part of the mentoring process. If you have decided on a career path you want to pursue, find someone who has been there to give you a clear picture of what that career path looks like. It may encourage you or it may do the opposite—convince you that career is not what you dreamed it could be.

Yogi Berra said in one of his Yogi-isms, "When you come to a fork in the road, take it." In a mentoring relationship, you may realize that not all of your goals will come to pass, and its best to not hang on too tightly to them. When new information or circumstances present themselves to you and you feel like you are at a crossroad, ask your mentor and pray for direction. Usually these prayers are answered by an opportunity to do something that might have never entered your mind. To talk things over and pray about it is step one, but at some point, a decision must be made. And the idea of "not making a decision is a decision in itself" is a fallacy.

Imagine what kids from bad-culture homes would gain by seeking a good mentor instead of getting into the wrong crowd and ending up in a world of trouble. At this summer-youth stage of life (let's say from teenager to 24) minds and core values might be established but are still like willow trees, bending and changing more easily. It's never too late to have a mentor, but it's not so easy for the old oak trees to bend and change.

The two major decisions made poorly during this period are decisions on faith in Jesus Christ and choice of a spouse. These two decisions are milestones in life. Many people make poor choices on the second choice (choosing a life partner) because they have bypassed the #1 priority, faith and core values. A bad marriage can ruin your life. Don't choose someone to live with the rest of your life based on good looks and charm. Find out what their values and dreams are. If your dreams and their dreams or your values and their values are far apart and are not compatible, put the relationship on hold and find out how tightly they hold those values and how motivated they are to pursue their dreams.

A young woman Gladys and I know married a fine young man. The marriage seemed to be a good fit for both. Their upbringings were similar, and their faith and values seemed on par with each other. However, after they were married for a while, it became very obvious their hopes and dreams for the future differed greatly. Long story short, they parted ways. That's the importance of knowing what your dreams are and making sure your partner's dreams are in sync with yours.

Times have changed drastically since I was in this summer of life. The worst offenses we committed were having muscle cars that (we thought) defined who we were, and we drove like maniacs. Plus we smoked a few cigarettes just because we thought it was cool. Today's vices are booze, drugs, and sex—and not knowing or caring how these will affect our future. Higher education carries much responsibility for this because young people are being taught that right and wrong are no longer black and white and we now live in a gray world where each one must choose what's right for them as individuals. **This is nothing less than tutoring from hell and will lead people to places that will harm and destroy them.**

Remember Decision #1; choosing correctly will negate this type of lifestyle. With faith comes wisdom and discernment. We will know what is right, what is wrong, and what is borderline.

Education can be a blessing, but it can also be a curse. Many of our youth today might have been raised by Christian parents, attended church, and are now ready to look at education they need for their career plans—*if* they need formal education to achieve their goals. Many are the trades that need no further education but offer countless opportunities. However, for those whose vocation does call for another four years of learning, many dangers lurk in our colleges. As a nation, we have been invaded by evil and harmful teachings that are deceiving many of our youth today. The influence of anti-God professors seeks to embed in young and impressionable minds beliefs that are not biblical and that claim the Bible is an archaic document no longer culturally relevant. Our country's culture is changing, condoning evil and scoffing at biblical principles on which our country was founded.

How do we counteract such brainwashing and garbage? One of the programs for young people today that will ground them firmly in truth and character is a program called OneLife. This is a nine-month discipleship program that not only educates (students earn college credits) but helps young people grow in their faith and character, in serving others, and in learning to live in community.

On their website, they state: "At OneLife, we know in order to grow in character you must first truly examine who you are becoming. In fact, we think it's more valuable to focus on who you are becoming rather than where you are going. This is the idea of character before a career." I would highly recommend this program for your son or daughter, whether or not they are planning to go to college. It's a tremendous foundational experience that will set them on a course for success.

OneLife has four locations: Pleasant View in Manheim Pennsylvania; Three Spring Ministries in Morris, Pennsylvania; Sakanaga in Marietta, South Carolina; and Lodestar Mountain Inn in Upper Tract, West Virginia. The Lodestar location is the Wilderness Campus, and it is the farm that we purchased for Wingfield Ministries for their retreat. OneLife now has dorms and a learning center there as well. For more information, go to onelifepath.org.

When I see what is happening with OneLife students, I regret that I didn't have this type of learning experience when I was in the summer season of my life. I could have avoided much pain and many regrets in my autumn and winter.

This summer stage can be exciting, but it's a good idea to remember that the choices you make will affect the fall and winter of your life. Stephen Covey's Habit 2 is so relevant: "Begin with the end in mind." Our problem is that we think the season we are in will last forever. I would dare say that few people think of what they want to be said in their eulogy and then live their life to match that. The wise person does think about the future and what effect their choices today will have on tomorrow.

ஐ•ஐ

Autumn is a beautiful time of year, and it should be a great time in our lives as well.

For me, the middle-age years were all about raising a family and building our business, with lots of hard work and busy schedules. At this age, we have our health, strength, a sharp mind, and plenty of opportunities. And so, because I was still healthy enough to enjoy an active life, I also went on big game hunts for elk, caribou, sheep, moose, and bear. All in all, this season of life was my favorite.

If every young parent would know in the early days of marriage and child-rearing years the weightiness of who we are and how it will affect who our children will become, we would all take this season of life more seriously. Our character and walk with the Lord will shape the next generation. Getting this stage of life right will bear much great fruit and will have a bearing on how we will spend the next season of our life.

I watched our kids become young adults and get married and start their own families. Our son and daughter, Eugene and Jenny, are good parents. They are people of character and are firmly established as Christ followers. My wife Gladys did much of the day-to-day training and teaching them how to live and was a great example to them.

Gladys came from a family culture of hard work, God-fearing people, a happy family, and great memories. I, on the other hand, came from a very strict home with an authoritarian dad and lots of conflict. As much as I disliked this culture while I lived at home, it was what I knew, and I found myself, in this summer season, falling back into the same trap I had grown up in. And that is a danger that everyone coming from a bad culture home will need to beware of. Cultures have a way of repeating themselves, both the good and the bad. Early in our marriage, my wife looked at me one evening and said, "I didn't marry your father, so don't act like him." To say that her words hit me like a rock is an understatement. But I knew she was right, and it caused me to rethink how I responded to her and the kids from that day forward.

In my autumn season, work was very important to me. I wanted to build a company that could last the test of time and go from my leadership to continuing under someone else who would build even further on what I and my father had begun. My father laid a great foundation for us to grow on. I built the house that now sits on his foundation, and my nephew Jason Weaver is continuing to enlarge the house.

The autumn is also the time when our fortunes are usually made or lost. I know businessmen who built companies, made lots of money, thought they were invincible, and became proud and haughty. They lived the good life, or so it seemed, but their pride and arrogance caused them to finish life poorly.

For one thing, hobbies can turn into obsessions and our lives come to be centered around things that do not help our careers, our families, or our faith. Then we need to consider what might result from trading what got us to where we are for having fun with our buddies. We were not created to live a life free of work, family, and faith, and when we do, everything can come crashing down. Lost fortunes, lost marriages, and poor character will lead to a really tough winter of serious regrets.

Don't get me wrong, working hard and making money is a great thing to do in this autumn season. The real question is what will we do with our money and what will it do to us. Jesus' words in Luke 12:48 (ESV) tell us, "To whom much is given, much will be required." In response to this, Casey Duhart wrote:

> If you have heard that line of wisdom, you know it means we are held responsible for what we have. If we have been blessed with talents, wealth, knowledge, time, and the like, it is expected that we benefit others.[5]

---

[5] Originally published in Tennessee Law, Spring 2016.

Doing exactly this will bring us great joy and favor. Benefitting others in many ways has great rewards, and when it comes right down to the end, what else matters? C.T. Studd wrote "Only one life, 'twill soon be past, Only what's done for Christ will last." These are two lines from a long poem he wrote. Google it and read it. It's very thought provoking.

As we enter the next and final season of life on Earth, we see that these lines accurately portray the reality of our numbered days here.

ꕥ♦ꕥ

I am quite familiar with the season of **winter.** I am living it now. We are enjoying its benefits: less stress; we can make our own schedule and leave more space for free time; no one reports to me anymore; we are still reasonably healthy (but with a fair number of aches and pains). Having replaced nearly every moving part of my skeletal structure over the past 15 years, I am hoping the warranty on these man-made parts will see me through to the end. We also can share with causes that are near and dear to us, and when I meet with people looking for free advice, I really don't care if they follow my advice or not. I am still involved in some business ventures, but not the day-to-day activities. That's the good news of the winter season.

The bad news is that our bodies are wearing out, our vision dimming, our memory shrinking. Joints hurt, and our body reminds us that it was not made to last forever. The chance to travel and see the things we always wanted to see is dependent on our health and wellbeing. For many, the winter season is a curse because of many ailments and pain, but it wasn't meant for that. Winter was meant to be a time of establishing our legacy and preparing for the life hereafter.

I think **our Creator designed us to be productive in all seasons of life** but in varying ways at different times. Instead of being large and in charge in this season, we are meant to be in a supportive role, where our life experiences have a big impact on those who are just encountering some of life's hurdles. With a steady hand and 70 years of living, we can be stability and encouragement to the next generation. The help we can offer to our families and friends in terms of advice is another gift we can give.

As grandparents, we can play a vital role in the lives of our grandchildren. Parents are busy, and a young child's inquisitive and persistent ways can become irritating. In contrast, grandparents are intrigued and fascinated watching these youngsters go from toddlers to school kids. For children, having wise and gentle grandparents can be a stabilizing factor in their young, impressionable lives.

None of my kids had much interest in hunting, fishing, or the great outdoors—those things I've loved all my life. But one of our four grandsons is an outdoor enthusiast and loves almost all things outdoors, including hunting. This year, I was with Reagan, age 10, when he harvested his first whitetail deer. What a thrill for him and Grandpa. Our long waits in the winter deer blinds made for some fun and interesting talks. I am so very grateful that I can pass on some of my lifetime experiences to him in my favorite settings out in the woods on our farm.

If you think children will soon forget these times and you question the importance of these precious moments, then think back to when you were ten years old. Our minds retain almost all memorable moments. Our memories are like an onion, layer upon layer. The last to go are the layers at the very inside of the onion. I could tell you in detail some of my highlights as a youngster. What happened last week or last year is a dim and foggy memory for me today.

Giving of our time to the next generation is a large part of our legacy. It's as important as what we give monetarily to great ministries. We help to write the stories of their lives.

We are not a threat to these dear young souls when we give good advice. Quite the opposite. These young, open minds are receptive, and today's kids are smart. There is almost no technology that they can't figure out. But the reality is that they are exposed to the vilest forms of humanity that no kid at any age should be exposed to. Common Sense Media Survey says that the average age kids are exposed to pornography is 12 years old.[6] Grandma and Grandpa can warn them about these dangers. Yes, the parents should be doing it, but grandparents have an obligation to warn as well. The devil's theory is that the younger he can ensnare these kids, the better chance he has in keeping them.

The most important counsel is this: **Our older years will in large part be a mirror of how we have lived the other three seasons of our lives**. Our pastor has said, "If you were an angry young person and you haven't made any major changes in your life, you will become an even more angry older person. If you were a kind and loving person as a youth, you will be an even kinder, more loving older person." You get the drift. Life without changes made for the good will simply accentuate characteristics in winter. Bitterness, unforgiveness, and broken relationships will cause us to have a bitter, lonely end. So, to an extent, we get to choose our winter season.

---

[6] https://www.commonsensemedia.org/press-releases/new-report-reveals-truths-about-how-teens-engage-with-pornography accessed April 12, 2023

I also believe that the last season of life brings great opportunities. In business, we can bring a tremendous amount of good as we serve on boards (if that's something we enjoy) because our experiences equip us for most situations. We can be culture warriors by simply living our lives as an example to those around us. Even though our memories dim and it's hard to remember names from one day to the next, our long-term memory is the last to go. The mistakes I made over the years I remember as if they were yesterday. I also remember the victories, and my creative thinking is as active as ever. We can always be looking to improve what we are involved in. Spotting problems and being proactive in solving them sooner rather than later has become a way of life for me that will last for the rest of my life.

One of the areas where I fall short is that because I am an introvert, I really don't enjoy public speaking, even though I have done quite a bit of this over the years. This thought hit me just yesterday as I was driving home from a business meeting: *If this is a gift and talent that God has given me and people still ask me to speak, I should share the wisdom that God has blessed me with.* If you don't like what I have to say, don't ask me to come back. I truly believe that each of us will be required to give an account of what we did with the gifts and talents our Creator gave us. That includes our occupation, as well as the influence He gave us.

In this final season, I am quite content to be where I am. I really wouldn't want to go back and relive any part of my life. My faith is stronger than ever, and I know where my future will be spent; it will be in the presence of the Almighty God. Anything we have experienced in life will pale in comparison to the glory that awaits those who have chosen Jesus as their Savior and have lived a life that honored Him. For the years I have left, I want to be an influence that will lead people to follow in His footsteps.

Our older years will in large part be a mirror of how we have lived the other three seasons of our lives.

Trust in the L*ORD* *with all your heart;*
do not depend on your own understanding. Seek his will in all you do,
and he will show you which path to take.

—Proverbs 3:5, 6

Chapter 11

Making Wise Decisions and Choices

The formula for making wise choices and decisions is perfected in these two verses in Proverbs. The author, King Solomon, gave all the credit for his good choices and decisions not to his own wisdom and understanding but to the God who gave him his wisdom.

Life is not an interstate highway but a series of roads that must be navigated wisely. Twisting and bumpy and sometimes CLOSED, these roads are not the smoothest and fastest way from Point A to Point B. They are also not by any means the easiest, but they are designed to teach us how hardships, delays, or even illness can guide us into the path that is best for us in the end. **Our choices and decisions are the steering wheel by which we maneuver down life's roads.**

Our choices and decisions shape our lives, our core values, and ultimately the culture we set in place for our families and businesses. Making good choices and decisions does not happen by chance or luck. This is a learned discipline. And the most brilliant decision makers are the students of Proverbs 3:5, 6. They understand that we are mere mortals and at best we can have a clear picture of the present, but none of us can predict the future, and that's the power of these verses in Proverbs. God alone can accurately predict the future and keep us from making poor decisions based on assumptions that may never come true.

I have been accused of quite a number of things, some true and some not true. But I don't recall anyone ever accusing me of being indecisive or a procrastinator. With age and experience, my decision making has become more methodical and a bit more regimented, but that doesn't mean that I put off making a decision for an extended period of time.

"The Art of Decision" is on a plaque hanging in my office. I received it from my coworkers.

THE ART OF DECISION
Decision is the spark
that ignites action.
Until a decision is made
nothing happens.
Decision is the courageous
facing of the issues.
It is focusing the powers of
intelligence, meditation and prayer
on the thing to be decided.
A decision need not
always be made at once.
Deciding to delay making
a decision is a decision in itself.
Decision awakens the spirit of man.
The great decision comes first,
the great work follows.
—Unknown

As one line reads, "Until a decision is made nothing happens." And that's why poor decision makers will say no to almost everything if risk is involved. Risk and fear are tight companions in decisions. Fear itself is a natural instinct and should be considered in making decisions, but fear left unchecked brings paralysis that blocks decisions that need to be made. Few attributes will take the wind out of a leader's sails faster than not being able to make timely decisions. Making clear, confident decisions is characteristic of strong leaders. A leader's decisiveness energizes their team and signals courage, competency, wisdom, and experience, all of what makes their people feel secure and increases the leader's influence.

Many opportunities are passed up by simply not moving fast enough. As Leonard Ravenhill points out, "The opportunity of a lifetime needs to be seized during the lifetime of the opportunity." I know this to be true, and that is why we need to be prepared to quickly shift our thinking from maintaining the status quo to making sometimes major decisions in a timely manner.

Over the years, Bobb Biehl's list of questions to ask ourselves has helped me look through the fog and get clarity when making a decision:

1. At its essence, in one sentence, what decision am I facing? What is the "bottom, bottom" line? Who, what, when, where, why, how, how much?
2. Have I given myself 24 hours to let this decision settle in my mind? Am I thinking about this decision with a clear head, or am I fatigued to the point where I shouldn't be making major decisions? Do I have "peace of mind" as I pray about it, and look at it from God's eternal perspective?
3. What would happen if we did not do what we are planning to do?

4. What difference will this decision make, 5-10-50-100 years from now?
5. What are the key assumptions we're making? What do we assume it will really cost? What do we assume will be its real benefits?
6. How will this decision affect our overall Masterplan? Will it get us off track or speed us along our way?
7. Should we seek outside counsel on this decision? How do our spouses and families feel about this decision? Have we checked references? Have we actually interviewed previous users of the product or service? (Have we done our due diligence?)
8. What are our very best one to three options? Can the big decision be broken into sub-parts and lower risk decisions be made at a few "go, no go" points along the way?
9. Is this what we would do if we had twice the budget? ... Half the budget? ... Five times as much time? ... A tenth the time? ... Twice as many staff people? ... Half as many staff?
10. Is this the best timing? If not now, when? Why not? If someone held a loaded gun to my head and forced me to decide in the next two minutes, what would I decide? Why?

These ten questions and our answers will add clarity to the issues we're facing and help us finalize our decision.

ꟸ♦ꟹ

One of the most important decisions we must make concerns charitable giving: How much do we give? Where do we give it? Who or what organization do we trust to use it in a wise way that brings maximum results?

Now, I have made my share of poor decisions regarding this issue, and here is what I have found to be helpful—

First, don't give money or your time impulsively. Think about it. Pray about it. Research the organization. A good place to start is on the website *Charity Navigator*. It has a wealth of information that will bring much clarity to the choice you are about to make.

The first question to always ask about a nonprofit is how much of their total revenue hits the ground and what percentage goes toward operations. The latter will usually include the salary of the president of the organization as well as the overall cost to run operations. *Charity Navigator* has a rating system, and the best-rated are at or close to 10 percent going toward operation expenses, which means nearly 90 percent goes toward their mission and vision. When nonprofits are at this level, it's obvious that a good portion of their operations are done by volunteers. This is a reliable sign of a well-run and good-culture entity. Who wants to volunteer for a group that has a poor culture?

Another big decision to be made in our giving is to establish a target amount for a year and then figure out how to budget around that number. This decision should not be made out of fear or a sense of duty but out of gratitude and cheerfulness. I mean, think about it. **We are able to invest in the work of the Kingdom, where our returns will be higher than any other available investment and will not be cyclical, as are the investments we make in the markets.** If that isn't enough reason to invest cheerfully in the Kingdom, compare the length of returns made in the financial markets. At best, companies can survive and be profitable for anywhere from ten to one hundred years. Kingdom investments will bring earthly returns, but more importantly, they will live on after we die and continue throughout eternity. No worldly investment can touch those returns.

> Every life exists for one of two purposes: to fill a greed or to meet a need.
> —Bobb Biehl

ꗥ♦ꗤ

In leading our company, the most difficult decisions I have had to make dealt with people who weren't working out in the job they were hired for.

I believe that simply doing our due diligence before hiring will avoid most of these difficult situations. However, in today's employee shortage, not only do we hire out of desperation, but we tolerate things that will come back to bite us. No matter how desperate we are, letting our guard down on who we hire is still more costly than hiring the right people—those who fit the job and whose character and competency are where they should be. The cost of a bad decision that leads to a bad hire is enormous, and that's why the long-standing concept of hiring slowly and firing swiftly is so important.

Even so, these difficult decisions must be made in any business, and we are no exception. Out of the 1,700 people we hired during my time at Weaver Leather, only a very small percentage were let go. Some of those employees we asked to leave lacked good character, and either their influence was causing others to join in with their bad habits, or the toxic environment they created in their area caused others to leave.

To put off making this type of decision in a timely manner is to jeopardize the very well-being of the company. The longer we wait, the greater the damage. At some point when decisive action is not taken, our credibility as a leader begins to erode, and as a result, people leave. I have learned that the sooner we nip problems in the bud, the sooner the culture will improve. I love this quote by Tony Robbins: "Whatever we tolerate, we get more of." So while some decisions can be postponed for a time, some need to be dealt with quickly.

In those cases where we had to let a person go, we first followed a sequence of decision points where the choice was the responsibility of the employee. When this progression was done right by the manager or the president, it worked well. Step one was to casually mention to the employee that they were breaking the terms they had agreed to in the hiring process, and they would be asked to not continue doing what they were doing. A time was set up to revisit the issue in the near future, a week or so later. At that appointed time, the manager would let the employee know that either a) they had made commendable positive improvement or, if there's been no change, b) they would be given one more chance to correct the issue and then if nothing changes, they will be asked to leave. This put 100 percent of the responsibility on the employee's shoulders. This procedure may not have made the employee feel any better if it came to dismissal, but it certainly made me feel better. By giving them a choice to make a positive decision, I always felt less remorse in having to do this.

ꟈ•ꟈ

Many of the bad decisions in our lives are made when we are young and simply inexperienced in how to do life. I tell many a young person that there are two fundamental decisions one must make that will affect them in years to come and possibly for a lifetime. Wise choices on these issues are paramount for living a successful, happy, and fulfilling life. The first and foremost is making a personal decision to accept Jesus Christ as our Lord and Savior and renounce sin and ungodly living. The second decision is choosing our life partner. This choice is critical; it will deeply affect our happiness and long-term joy and fulfillment. An unwise decision can be detrimental and even destructive to our future. A bad marriage affects you, your kids, and your ability to focus on your goals and endeavors.

Decision #1 should be made before entering into Decision #2. Our filter for all decisions will change when our hearts are right with our heavenly Father. If you use society's current template for making this decision, you'll get it all wrong.

The accepted version today for finding your life partner is to live together and "test the waters" to see if this is the right partner for you. Nothing could be more wrong. The blame can again be laid at the doorstep of today's churches. A great many churches never talk about the sanctity of marriage and the consequences that follow when the written Word is ignored.

The Bible is very clear about God's plan for marriage. It is between a husband and a wife, to be lived in a monogamous relationship for as long as they live. That is His perfect plan. His plan was violated even back in the days when Jesus walked and taught here on Earth, thousands of years ago, but it was and is still His plan. And it's for our own good.

It is quite interesting that science has actually "caught up" with what the Bible says. Secular research now is finding that couples who marry without having cohabited have a lower rate of divorce. *Not* living together prior to marriage is still the wisest choice for couples; waiting to cohabit until married tends to strengthen a marriage, not weaken it. So even though modern-day culture prescribes doing most everything in a non-Biblical and secular way, the facts remain that following Jesus' teachings will always pay off with big rewards.

ꟹ•ꟹ

As "The Art of Decision" states, making important decisions is "focusing the powers of intelligence, meditation, and prayer on the thing to be decided." **Prayer might well be the most powerful tool in our arsenal when we're faced with difficult decisions.** It is when we realize that God's power is upon us that we become dependent on Him to answer our prayers and bring clarity, discernment, and the right people at just the right time to make our decisions successful.

For a number of years now, I've been involved in a food market. At one time, we were pondering a decision of whether to add a bakery to the market instead of just buying the products from other bakeries at their wholesale prices—a practice that left us with very thin margins and did not always give us the quality we wanted for our customers.

Now, our area has many bakeries, and it seemed like a big risk for us to also get into the business. We had no experience with this, and with so many very good bakeries around, prices were already very competitive. We were doubting the wisdom of adding our own bakery products

Through a series of negative events, I came in contact with one of our vendors who supplied us with fry pies. Fry pies are an Amish staple in this area, and we sell large quantities of them. In conversation with this vendor, he and I realized that our dads had worked together many years ago, and I'd often heard his dad's name come up at home. We'd established a connection, and I told him about the decision we were facing regarding starting our own bakery.

He mentioned that they had a neighbor who, due to health issues, was looking for a buyer for her little bakery. He mentioned that her recipes were very good and her breads, cookies, and coffeecakes were topnotch in quality. Long story short, we ended up buying the bakery and her equipment and recipes. More importantly, the ladies who were doing her baking were willing to help us set up our new bakery. They spent quite a few days educating our people in the art of baking and sharing all the little secrets they had learned by trial and error over the years.

As a result, we now have a thriving bakery that produces some of the best baked goods in our area. Our customers are delighted and show their gratitude by buying large quantities of our delicacies every week. If you're ever in our area in Berlin, Ohio, look us up at Troyer Market. We would love to have you sample our baked goods.

The point is that through a series of events we were led into this opportunity that solidified our decision. Happenings like this strengthen my resolve to always pray before making difficult decisions.

ꕥ

The only thing worse than not making decisions in a timely manner or making bad decisions is making a bad decision and finding out that we made a bad decision and then continuing to beat the dead horse because we are too proud to admit that we made a bad decision. Sound crazy? It is, but on many occasions, I have seen so-called leaders do exactly that. Pride and ego say "If you just stick with it, things will eventually work themselves out."

Now, not all decisions need to be completely aborted. Usually, a few obvious changes will take us down a better path. But for some leaders, changing anything becomes a reflection on their judgment and decision-making ability, and rather than admit there were flaws in the original plan and having the guts to admit it was their idea that ended up in rigor mortis, they will, as a last-ditch effort to save face, blame someone else for the disastrous results. I have zero tolerance for these obstinate, prideful leaders.

Our political leaders are masters at this. Even when we hear the sound bites of what they said and the decisions they made, they will blatantly blame someone else from the other political party for the carnage created. If these people were employed by the private sector, they would be on the street, looking for handouts. The culture over the past one hundred years has declined to the point that they can and will pass laws that protect them from repercussions when they make poor choices, and no one will hold them accountable.

Folks, our government is corrupt. There are many people in dark places making decisions that continually hurt our country. Even though we have a two-party system, justice is not being served, and power has tilted in favor of evil men who will do what it takes to gain absolute power and who are looking to destroy what our forefathers established and shed their blood for.

I am 70 years old, and without a miracle from God, my children's children will live in a world where freedom to live, to worship, and to confront evil will be gone, all because we have allowed people who make poor decisions to remain in office for a lifetime and as a country have not held them accountable for their deeds.

We have a dire warning, and we need to take it to heart. Exactly who said this first is under debate, but it's often been quoted, and it's true in any country and in any time: "The only thing necessary for the triumph of evil is for good men to do nothing."

Today, there are millions of good, God-fearing people who have taken the path of least resistance. When we choose that pathway, we make decisions based on how to best avoid conflict in our lives, our jobs, our churches, and our government. Taking that path allows evil to succeed, and it will lead to the certain demise of the greatest country on Earth.

If avoiding conflict is the correct pathway for mankind, then Jesus' life and His example was meaningless. Neither He nor His disciples would have been persecuted and executed if they'd chosen that path. But they spoke the truth in boldness no matter what the consequences, and most of them died a martyr's death. You see, they made the right decision long before they were thrown into prison and tortured for their words. They took the road of *most resistance*. They did this, knowing full well what the outcome would be, and they did it because they were sold out to their cause, which was more important than preserving their own lives.

Totally non-offensive the Bible is not. The very name of Jesus has an effect on other religions, the elites who lead our governments, our media, and many of our wealthiest, best-educated people. No other name could evoke such cynicism, skepticism, and downright hatred. And the reason is simple. In a world of no absolutes, His teachings are absolute. Today's theology is that God is whoever you think He is and the Bible is looked at as archaic and no longer relevant. I disagree. The Bible shows us how God deals with our sin and how Jesus changed our relationship to God. Before Jesus' day, the forgiveness of sins was only through real sacrifices. Jesus' death on the cross covers our sins *if* we believe in Him and have made Him the Lord of our life.

☙•❧

On September 29, 1982, three people in the Chicago area died after taking cyanide-laced Tylenol. This was the outset of a poisoning spree that would claim the lives of seven people in just two days. Forty years later, the evildoer has never been found.

In less than 24 hours after the first deaths, Tylenol willingly removed $100 million worth of these painkillers from shelves worldwide. When asked why they made such a costly decision so quickly, they said they had decided early on that their values were more important than money and people mattered more than anything else. Instead of this crisis completely crippling them, it made heroes out of their leadership.

This was a decision made by people who had decided in advance they wanted to do the right thing no matter what. Very few people will be forced to make a decision that would affect this many people and cost this amount of money, but what if we were forced to do something we knew was wrong and that could have catastrophic consequences in the long run? Would we really sacrifice our lives because of a decision we've made?

We can and should make this decision ahead of time: that whatever happens we will speak truth and represent our God and Savior well.

The importance of making good decisions with prayer and discernment has never been more critical. One thing is painfully clear: The masses are turning away from Jesus and His teachings. (The masses are never a good example to follow.) As history will show, more and more people are finding their own ideas about their future were inaccurate and are deciding that Christians are the cause of all calamity.

The Bible is very clear about the end times of this earth and how events will unfold. In a millisecond, God is going to miraculously rapture His church, removing them from this world. Those left behind will be forced to receive the mark of the beast, a small microchip that could be planted under the skin of the forehead or the right arm. Without this identification, no one will be able to buy or sell anything, and those not complying will be executed. Those who take the mark will be lost to eternal damnation known as hell. The ruler of that time will be the antichrist and will rule over all the earth.

So when will these events take place? My dad was sure he would see the rapture of the church, but he didn't. The exact day and time no one knows except the Father, God Himself. However, He does give us concise indicators of the season. It's like the four seasons of the year. We know that when the leaves turn, it is fall; when the snow falls, it is winter; when the trees start to bud, it is springtime; and when the temps reach 80 degrees and the days are long, it is summer. Jesus said we'd know the season by the signs. All the prophecies have been fulfilled, the country and world are turning away from God at a free-fall rate, and the stage is set for a one-world government. I firmly believe we are seeing all the signs of the last days. For believers, our redemption draws near. For unbelievers, their worst nightmare will be reality when they are faced with the choice of receiving the mark of the beast or putting their lives on the line for their choices. To live in a state of preparedness is the key to living in peace. Personally, I long to see the rapture of Christ's church. The older I get, the more I realize that this world is not my home.

ꕥ

Ultimately, we are all held accountable for the decisions and choices we make. Yes, there is forgiveness for the bad choices, but I have come to recognize that even though we are forgiven, the penalties still follow us, some for the rest of our lives. The law of sowing and reaping is still very much in effect today: "Don't be misled—you cannot mock the justice of God. You will always harvest what you plant" (Galatians 6:7). So there are no free passes for making poor choices and decisions. Just because no one has learned our dirty little secrets doesn't mean that the all-seeing eyes of God have not seen every little devious decision we have made.

But He also rewards our good decisions. That's why those verses from Proverbs 3 (at the beginning of this chapter) are so very important. He never gives us bad advice or weak wisdom; His direction is always spot on—if we care to ask. If I am not certain about a decision, I pray that He would either close the door and say *No*, or open doors and say *Yes*. I then accept the answer and move on it.

Prayer and asking has worked countless times for me and it will work for you as well. Try it! But be prepared; you may not get the answer you wanted.

Procrastination is one of the most common and deadliest of diseases, and its toll on success and happiness is heavy.

—Wayne Gretzky

Chapter 12

The Road to Nowhere

My dad was the ultimate get-'er-done person. He had a little saying: "Get off your knees and hustle, this is the Promised Land!" I learned early on that any job on the to-do list of the day left undone would be added onto the following day's list, and that day's undones added to the next day, until a day of reckoning when all would need to be done in one single day.

The greatest enemy of achievement is procrastination, the avoidance of doing something. The advanced and skilled procrastinator reasons that "I am gathering information" or "I am still praying about this" or even "There is no urgency in this matter." **But excuses are the guise under which this thief of time and progress operates and turns talented people into unproductive failures.**

In the workplace, procrastination wreaks havoc on the culture. Few things sap a good culture faster than an indecisive or procrastinating leader. Good people leave because they're looking for a leader who is decisive and moves the ball forward; people lose respect for a leader who refuses to make timely decisions. Lack of urgency at the top will resonate throughout the company, and widespread apathy puts a negative set to the culture of the company.

Let's extend this to the culture of a family. Suppose Mom and Dad mention the fact that a Florida vacation over the kids' spring break would be nice. Months pass, both parents are busy, and the vacation doesn't look as alluring as it did when they first mentioned it. By the time they look at housing, airline tickets, and costs, they decide to scrub the idea. The kids are devastated by the news and feel betrayed. If that type of procrastination and broken promises occur repeatedly, the kids lose their confidence in and respect of their parents.

Only the lazy and unmotivated workers embrace procrastination. A high-performing team doesn't have a place for procrastinators. A good team will only cover for someone for a little time before putting enough pressure on them to cause them to move on. Our goal at Weaver Leather was to ship 99 percent of all orders complete and on time in 24 hours. Doing this left no room for procrastinators. Period. They simply got run over and left on their own, or they were let go. A high-performing team simply cannot tolerate a procrastinator.

Whether in business or personal life, procrastinators will not be successful. The opportunities we encounter must be acted on in a timely manner or, many times, they disappear. When I need to make a decision very quickly, I use Bobb Biehl's suggestion to imagine someone holding a gun to my head (see Chapter 11). I have three seconds to make this decision before the gun goes off. The mind will spit out the answer in a second, and it's usually right. I have seen people agonizing their next move in a card game. Their indecision is based on not knowing what the other people hold in their hands, so they waffle, tap their fingers on the table, and force everyone to wait for their decision. If the three-second gunshot would apply, all of these people would be dead. In a couple of days, no one will remember who won or lost the card game; it's not important and not worthy of more than three seconds of our time.

ᘓ•ᘐ

Every day in the workplace, snares can tempt us to procrastinate. Most day-to-day decisions where the answer is obvious can and should be made immediately; others can be made within a couple of days or a week. The key is to set a time and date to finalize the decision or action.

Decisiveness will build your team's confidence in you, their leader. And little things do matter. If someone brings a complaint to you, the manager, like unclean bathrooms, cheap and horrible-tasting coffee, or unsanitary conditions in the workplace, if you're a wise manager, you'll take care of it *now.* Your people won't have to go up the totem pole to get it fixed. Bottom line: If you respect their logical request, they will respect your logical request.

In more weighty and more risky decisions, procrastination is often rationalized as *caution*. What-ifs can stop progress dead in its tracks.

Gladys and I took a vacation to celebrate our fiftieth anniversary. We went to Maine to see the beauty of the Northeast. One of the many sights are the old lighthouses that dot the coastline. We visited quite a number of these historic sites and they all had one thing in common: a lengthy circular staircase that led to the top where the light was located. With a bum knee, I could have yielded to *what if... What if my knee gives out? What if the climb makes the pain even worse and ruins the rest of our vacation? What if I get up there, and it wasn't worth the effort?* But the key to appreciating the entire experience was to take the first step and then the next and the next, and before we knew it, we were at the top, looking out over a large expanse of the Atlantic Ocean. Those views will always be etched in my mind. It was worth the climb.

It's the first step that stops people from experiencing success. I mean, what was the worst thing that could happen? We could have always turned around and gone back if the old knee gave out, but guess what? It didn't. And that's the way life is.

Sometimes the answer is not apparent until we take the first step. And the good news is that even when we reach an obstacle that is insurmountable, there's usually a detour we can take that will get us to the goal. Many of life's obstacles are unseen and will slow us down, but only on the rare occasion will we need to turn around and backtrack to where we started. We will nearly always be able to find a way around the obstacles and continue on.

The what-ifs represent risk, but the greater the risk, the greater the reward could be. In my tenure at Weaver Leather, we were constantly looking for ways to move us ahead, be it automation, technology, new buildings, or acquisition. All came at a cost not only of money but of stretching our team and all of us getting out of our comfort zone. When someone had a great idea that could move the company forward, there was a risk. There was also a reward to be gained. Our methodology behind making the decision to move ahead was quite simple.

First, as an executive group of four or five people, we had already agreed that there was merit in pursuing this opportunity. We'd done some of the due diligence and research needed before we presented it to a larger group.

Then we called a meeting of everyone who was going to be affected by the decision. The size and the scope of the decision determined how many people were involved in the vision casting. Those in the executive group were the advocates who gave our best pitch to get everyone on board. We gave the best-case and worst-case scenarios and then opened the discussion to the expanded group of people.

We encouraged people to pick apart the idea and share their concerns and what they saw as potential pitfalls if we moved forward. In this conversation, it was extremely important to answer any questions that would bring "buy in" from the group. Dissent and concerns were always—and I do mean *always*—voiced by one or two people, usually from our accounting department. Some concerns were valid, some were not, but it was important that all were heard and given time to express their concerns.

If there was additional fact finding to be done, the right people were assigned to get all the facts they could. Now I realize none of us will ever get 100 percent of the information we would like to have on any decision. If we did, the decision would pose almost no risk. So we considered it good if we got 50 to 60 percent of the vital info needed.

Before this meeting ended, we set up a follow-up meeting to finalize and go over any new information we received. In this next meeting, a decision would be reached to move forward or to abort. Normally, when everyone was heard, we'd analyzed new information, and we concluded we could overcome the unknowns, the decision would be unanimous to move ahead.

If we decided to go forward, I asked each person if they were prepared to throw in their full support, even though some had misgivings. I wanted to be certain no one would try to sabotage the process because of their concerns.

When the decision was *Go!*, the wheels went into motion, and unless someone brought forth new information that could damage our company, no one had the right to speak negatively to the others in the group or anyone outside the group. All concerns and roadblocks were handled by the executive team, CEO, CFO, COO, or VP of Sales, with the final decisions in the hands of the president and CEO.

This entire process might have taken a month or more. The weightier and riskier a decision, the more time this process may take. That's not procrastination; procrastination is delaying a decision for months without forward movement. This decision-making process is moving forward with prudence and well-thought-out preparation. The waiting period is called "actively waiting," doing what we can while waiting on pertinent information.

ഇ•ഠ3

Many of our prayers are wasted by our procrastination. God gives us wisdom to make good decisions, but when we continue to pray for the answer, it's like waiting for a text from God that tells us to get up and go, when He has probably put the opportunity in front of us in the first place.

When we read the Bible and see the commands God gave His chosen ones and the excuses some of them gave, we see this poisonous tic of procrastination has buried itself in our skin and infected the human race. The good news is that no one is stuck with this disease. Four principles will cure you of procrastination.

1. **Motivation** is the internal eagerness to act and attain goals. Developing motivation is easy, even if it's not your learned behavior. Fake it till you make it! Eventually you will start feeling a real sense of accomplishment and achievement, and being motivated will become a way of life. One class of people will not try this unless their life is endangered—the lazy who walk among us. They may be the second or third generation receiving and living on welfare, and the rest of our population's taxes are paying their way. Out of the millions who are using this as a way of life, a small handful are impaired, and those include the alcoholics and drug addicted as well. Scripture tells us to take care of our poor people, not those who are lazy. The Bible says if a man does not work, he should not eat. Hunger has a great way of getting people off their duff and working.

2. **Initiative** does what needs to be done without being asked. Waiting for further instructions can be a form of procrastination and being too apathetic to think for yourself. Lack of initiative equals slim opportunity to rise above mediocrity. The waiting game, unmoving till someone tells you what's next, is not rewarding and not rewarded.

3. **Decisiveness** is the principle of finalizing difficult decisions accurately and without hesitation. This is, to a certain extent, a talent that comes to some more naturally than others. It can be learned by making a mental assessment of the importance of the decision and how much thought should go into it, evaluating things like the worst thing that could happen and the best outcome you could hope for. We have been given a very sophisticated mind that works in ways no computer will ever match. So trust it. If you have put good and wise things into it, then it will give back good answers.

4. **Courage** is displayed when we feel the fear but do the right thing anyway, no matter the cost or the difficulty. Lack of courage may be the number one reason people procrastinate and waffle on decision making. I am reading through the four Gospels, Matthew, Mark, Luke, and John. The account of the last twenty-four hours of Jesus' life on this earth gives us a perfect picture of courage. He knew exactly what was going to happen in the hours after His last supper with His disciples. He was as human as we are but without sin. When Judas brought the mob to arrest Him, one of His disciples pulled out his sword and whacked off the ear of one of those who came. Jesus told him to put away the sword. He said those who use the sword will die by the sword. Matthew 26:53: "Don't you realize that I could ask my Father for thousands of angels to protect us, and he would send them instantly?" I would dare to say that nearly all of us would have called the 1-800-FATHER number and asked for the angels to come and get us out of this jam. But from the very beginning, Jesus had a choice to say yes or no. He had made the choice 33 years before, and nothing would deter him. That's courage.

Jesus did all of that for you and for me, my friend, and all we need to do to spend eternity with Him is accept Him as our risen Lord and Savior, turn from our wicked ways, and follow His teachings. If you are a procrastinator, I ask you to not procrastinate on this most crucial decision. Right now, wherever you are, get on your knees and pray this prayer:

> Heavenly Father, I come to You in prayer asking for the forgiveness of my sins. I confess with my mouth and believe with my heart that Jesus is Your Son and that He died on the cross at Calvary that I might be forgiven and have eternal life in the Kingdom of Heaven. Father, I believe that Jesus rose from the dead and I ask You right now to come into my life and be my personal Lord and Savior. I repent of my sins and will worship You all the days of my life! Because Your Word is truth, I confess with my mouth that I am born again, cleansed by the blood of Jesus! In Jesus' name, Amen.
> -- *The Sinner's Prayer*

This is the most important decision you will ever make. If you have earnestly prayed this prayer, these three things can take you to the next steps.

1. The book *How to Grow in Your Christian Faith* is available on Amazon for $8.95.
2. Buy the *NLT Life Application Bible Study Bible* and start by reading through the book of Ephesians.
3. Find a good Bible-teaching church and get into a fellowship with other believers.

Some might wonder why I included these paragraphs in this book on culture. The answer is simple. In our homes, businesses, and any other organization, our core values and character are what shape the culture. And our character and core values stem from this decision of simple faith. Folks, this is the most important part of this book.

A life and heart where God is absent will never produce the end results that a life committed to God will produce. It's virtually impossible. Jesus addressed this issue in Luke 6:45: "A good person produces good things from the treasury of a good heart, and an evil person produces evil things from the treasury of an evil heart." What we say and do will be consistent with our core values. Yes, for short periods of time, we can pretend to be someone we are not, but in the long-term, what is on the inside will come out. We deceive ourselves when we overlook the actions and words of someone, ignoring obvious signs of who they really are, because they are our friend and they can be quite charming at times. Many marriages have fallen by the wayside because one of them looked the other way when the signs and words clearly pointed out that the other person had never been fully committed to God and the marriage is divided. Or it may happen that a son or daughter "accepted Christ" as a small child, but as they grew up their life did not reflect a changed heart.

The invitation from God is not contingent on whether the "good" in your life outweighs the "bad." If that were the case, we would all be without hope. This decision is nothing more than acceptance of a holy God and giving Him the full reign of our lives. It's so simple, many people miss the mark and try to live a good moral life on their own power. That is futile because the old nature we were all born with is sinful. Every one of us needs a Savior to overcome our sin nature.

As a young person, we believe we have a long life ahead of us to make this decision and in the meantime we can live however we want, bide our time, and try to do more good than bad. But the human race has a 100 percent mortality rate and not one of us knows when we will draw our last breath. So to all of the world's procrastinators, don't wait to make this eternally important decision.

Christianity will survive without America, but America will not survive without Christianity and without the foundation of the Word of God.

—Jentezen Franklin

Chapter 13

Culture in the Homeland

Our country was founded by brave men and women 247 years ago on July 4, 1776, as a place of freedom from repressive governments. That freedom was the driving factor, and close on the heels of that purpose was the desire for freedom of religion where government would not interfere with one's beliefs and living out one's beliefs. Our founding fathers had a clear template of what the country ought not to be, as well as what they wanted it to be. The price to defend and to keep what they had instituted was high, and we became the target of those wishing to take over this country and its valuable resources.

Our constitution was brilliantly crafted and designed to put the power in the hands of the people, not the hands of a governing body. It was a republic for the people and by the people. Leaders were paid by the people and voted in or out of office by the people.

Our republic was never flawless, but it became the envy of the world. Our growth and our culture were like no other country, and we became the first world superpower. We also became the wealthiest country on the planet. The world community was baffled by our ingenuity, our resolve, and our culture.

What had grown out of July 4, 1776, was uncommon, and in 1831, just 55 years after our inception, two French men decided to pay a visit to this new and up and coming country to see what we did and, more importantly, how we were doing things that their country had never been able to accomplish. The man in charge of researching and documenting our progress was Alexis de Tocqueville; his companion and fellow traveler was Gustave de Beaumont. They spent ten months traveling across the developed parts of our country in hopes of taking home the secrets to the success we were experiencing. Their search for answers took them from towns and cities to farms, factories, and every facet of life in the United States. They also took special interest in our government and how it had been set up to give the power back to the people and to do so with a minimum amount of government. De Tocqueville was baffled by the philanthropic culture where business and government worked together to build infrastructure, factories, hospitals, prisons, and churches. This joint effort and the resulting accomplishments were quite different from his country, where the tax dollars were spent and used by the government and the private sector had very little say as to how funds were used. His country lacked the synergy we had developed, of business and government working together for the common good of all the people.

Even though de Tocqueville documented many things, he still was dumbfounded at the results he was seeing. Yes, the people were industrious and hardworking, and farms and factories were doing well, but his findings still didn't explain the true mystery of our dynamic culture and our growth and prosperity. He saw both the good and the bad, such as slavery and the mistreatment of Native Americans. Before he left to go back to France, he had one more sector of our culture he wanted to research, and these are his famous words:

> Not until I went into the churches of America and heard her pulpits flame with righteousness did I understand the secret

> of her genius and power. America is great because America is good, and if America ever ceases to be good, America will cease to be great.

Over the next 191 years, we managed to do exactly what de Toqueville had predicted.

Comparing the percentage of believers to non-believers in our country, we are still in decline. The claim of many is that the "great cultural divide" results because intolerant Christians will not leave the teachings of the Bible out of our society, and this divide would be resolved if it weren't for "religion" which (as they would say) has no place in our schools or in state and federal government. Some churches denounce sin and immorality, and that's being "judgmental." In the minds of unbelievers, the Bible is full of inconsistencies and should not, cannot, be used as our moral compass.

As a nation, we have slowly but surely taken our eyes off what has made us good and great. Our wealth, self-sufficiency, and power have corrupted the very roots of our homeland. The core values that created the great culture de Tocqueville witnessed have been compromised and changed. Every sector that could be infiltrated by this deviation has been subverted. Our schools have gone from the best to, in some cases, the worst. Instead of preparing our young people for the future, "educators" are indoctrinating children to hate our country and to accept sexual perversion as "normal" and "good." Were it not for Christian schools and homeschools and private schools, our people would have no choices.

Starting at an early age to warp a child's mind is the ultimate way to change the culture in our homeland. Every initiative our government is pushing on us is designed to bring down our country's economy, education, media, and health care.

And it's amazing that a small minority of our population is capable of changing what worked for over 200 years. Their goal is to go back to the very place our new republic paid such a high price to be free of—an autocratic government that controls our lives and wants to control our beliefs.

I wonder what Alexis de Tocqueville would say if he did his documentary today? His assessment was spot on. The presence of good and righteousness that comes from our faith in Jesus Christ has the power to keep evil at bay. It's like a light shining in a room, keeping out the darkness. But if that light is turned off, darkness immediately takes over. There is never a void; it is either light or darkness. So it is in our world; we are the light of the world, and without it, darkness and evil move in.

> "You are the light of the world—like a city on a hilltop that cannot be hidden. No one lights a lamp and then puts it under a basket. Instead, a lamp is placed on a stand, where it gives light to everyone in the house. In the same way, let your good deeds shine out for all to see, so that everyone will praise your heavenly Father in heaven." (Matthew 5:14-16)

The rise and fall of countries has been well documented over the last 6,000 years. When evil takes over, a country eventually comes to ruin. And that's the focal point that de Tocqueville came away with when he predicted that when America is no longer good, America will no longer be great.

ꙮ

In March of 2023, Marion County, Florida, and the entire country was shocked by the brutal murder of three juveniles by three other juveniles. Fox News reported an interview with Billy Woods, the sheriff of Marion County. Woods not only lamented of the loss of three young adults but also the harm that society is causing children who commit criminal activity. Woods said,

> "We're just degrading our society in these great United States in which you and I live. The failure here is the fact that we do not get to the root cause; family, our schools, and even ourselves out here in society. We, in fact, are enabling everything in which they do, just because we don't hold them accountable, just because we minimize their actions. We don't do them justice. We're doing them harm... There's nothing good in this scenario. You got six teens, which is ravaging not just my community, but it's ravaging every community across this nation where our youths are engaged in more criminal activity."[7]

The article noted that the Office of Juvenile Justice and Delinquency Prevention reports that since 2020, there has been a noticeable spike in crime committed by and against young adults. The increase in the number of children under the age of 14 committing crimes is the highest it's been in nearly two decades. In our nation's capital, juvenile deaths from gunfire in 2022 increased by 56% from the previous year.

> "People think that we, like myself, are hard. We have hearts. I have kids, and I understand in these scenarios. But the fact is, we dance around the issues. We want to focus on one thing [guns] that has no capability. I'm here to tell you that the gun didn't knock on their door, walk in their room and say 'hey,

---

[7] https://www.foxnews.com/media/fla-sheriff-degrading-american-institutions-root-cause-rising-violence-among-juveniles, accessed May 3, 2023

> look, let's go kill somebody today.' They [the teens] made a conscious decision."

Woods said we must hold these children accountable, but more importantly, parents need to be accountable for their children. He called for parents and schools to take more responsibility in raising up our children. Proverbs 22:6 is very clear about our responsibility as parents: "Direct your children onto the right path, and when they are older, they will not leave it." This verse puts the spotlight directly on us as parents, not the schools or government programs. The word *direct* (or *train,* in some translations) denote very intentional guidelines that need to be adhered to by the parents and our youth. To leave it up to our children to "find their own way" is the exact opposite of what needs to happen.

Woods added that America needs to return to its foundational values and seek social restoration to help the nation's youth and fix the issue at its root cause. "We need to go back to... our faith and our beliefs, back to our fathers that disciplined us. This is missing. It truly is. The foundation is there, but the walls have crumbled, and we need to build them back up."

How true Billy Woods's words are. The failures of our society and culture are a direct result of our core values.

ꙮ

As 2024 looms in the not-so-distant future and we go to the polls to select our next leaders, the request for money to support the candidate of our choosing is relentless. They promise that with the right people in power we can take back our country, return it to what it once was. In my opinion, that is delusional.

Our problem is not a political problem; it is a spiritual problem. We were founded on biblical principles, we were blessed like no other nation ever was before us, and now we have turned our back on what made us great and on the blessing.

The church in general has played a big role in our country's digression. Many church denominations have allowed sin into their churches in the name of inclusion. We hear only the portions of the Bible that teach love, forgiveness, and God's mercy toward us. The rest of the Scriptures are seldom or never mentioned. And that's why our pulpits today are not "flaming with righteousness."

Like a thief in the night, evil has crept into our culture. This quote accurately portrays where we are as a country today:

> First we overlook evil.
> Then we permit evil.
> Then we legalize evil.
> Then we promote evil.
> Then we persecute those who still call it evil.
> (Author unknown)

The penalty for not living a God-honoring life and repenting and accepting Him as our Lord and Savior is hell. It's not a curse word or a way for people to express their feelings. It is a real place where people will spend eternity. That's the rest of the story, folks. The gift and the penalty must both be explained to help people understand that a choice must be made by everyone. Not making the right choice is making the bad choice.

As our next election gains momentum, we should not think for one minute that our personal future and our country's future depend on election results. According to biblical prophecy, we are entering into an era that will lead to the end of the age and the second coming of Jesus Christ. No one can predict the day or the time accurately. But we do know the season we are in because of the warnings God left us in His inerrant Word, the Bible. All the things prophesied have come to pass, and the ending is well documented in Revelation. If you have never read through the book of Revelation, I urge you to do so. Use the New Living Translation or the New International Version to gain clarity on how this will happen. This subject is also not mentioned in many churches for fear it will drive people away and make them fearful. Fear itself is a great motivator. It keeps us from stepping off a building, jumping out of a plane without a parachute, or taking unnecessary risks.

As believers and Christ followers, we should not lose hope, because our redemption is drawing near. We may feel like we are losing every battle we fight, but the outcome and the victory will be ours. Guaranteed. He promised us that in the end, justice will be done. In the meantime, our job is to be a beacon of light and to build a good culture right where we are.

The greatest legacy one can pass on to one's children and grandchildren is not money or other material things accumulated in one's life, but rather a legacy of character and faith.

—Billy Graham

Chapter 14

Leaving a Legacy

When you think of people who have left a great legacy, who comes to mind? Take a few minutes and think about people you knew personally who accomplished great things that benefited many people. Now think of people you have never met who have impacted both your life and the lives of the masses. All except one of these were men and women just like you and I. The only person who was supernatural was Jesus. None of us will ever do for mankind what He did. Isn't it strange that the mention of His name can induce hatred and curses but for His followers it's the sweetest name on Earth.

What will your legacy be? *Legacy* is normally thought of as money left for a good cause, an inheritance, or a foundation that serves people long after the benefactor is gone. But money in itself is neutral. It can do horrific evil or it can bring life to many. Our core values will determine what we do with our money. If we are driven by self-gratification, the legacy dies when the last item we had is sold to the highest bidder.

Some of the greatest legacies are left by people who did not leave money but gave of themselves while they were living. A mother's care can create a legacy that goes on from generation to generation. A father's love and counsel can set up a young person for life. There are thousands of ways we can bless people in our lifetime. Think about it—where would we be without the words of wisdom shared with us by our friends, our business associates, our doctors, our accountants, or our attorneys? For some advice, we pay; some is free. But all the good advice is worth more than it costs us because we can then practice and use it for the rest of our lives. We are also expected to use what we have received, to pass it on and help our fellow man as well. The greatest gift we can give another is not monetary, but it is helping others who need a kind word of encouragement or words of wisdom and truth. We never know how far our words will go when given to a willing and receptive person.

Our legacy is what we will pass on to others, be it our faith, our core values, our ethics. Legacy is founded in character. None of us knows how many people are watching our lives. Good character is noticed, and our example can guide others and sometimes change the course of lives.

Our first commitment is to God and to be His light in a dark world. John Maxwell has always said that influence is the purest form of leadership. So influence done well will leave a great legacy.

Think about the influence Jesus had on those who met Him and sat under His teachings. None of us will ever do for mankind what He did. He healed the sick, raised people from the dead, and taught the truth. He was a humble man and always pointed people to His heavenly Father. He didn't have a home; He had no wealth. He was both loved and hated, and in the end, He was executed like a common criminal. Yet no human has ever left a greater legacy in our world. His legacy is that He cared for people in ways that no one has ever done before or since. So if we are to emulate this perfect legacy and ministry, shouldn't that be our model as well?

The Bible says three things will last forever—faith, hope, and love. And the greatest of the three is love (1 Corinthians 13:13). I can't think of a better formula for creating a lasting legacy.

Faith can be loyalty to someone we believe in. But our Christian *faith* is defined as showing "the reality of what we hope for; it is the evidence of things we cannot see. By faith we understand that the entire universe was formed by God's command, that what we now see did not come from anything that can be seen" (Hebrews 11:1, 3).

Hope is believing something good is going to happen. Hope is essential to our lives. Without hope we lose our way. Without hope, POWs would perish. Hope is what gets us up in the morning; it's what brings us out of bad times. When we share hope with others, it encourages them.

Love, the greatest of these three, is the most powerful tool whereby we can leave a great legacy. We can express our feelings in many ways, but when we tell someone we love them and then show our love by our actions, it is undoubtedly the greatest gift we can give. Few things are stronger than the bond created by love.

If these three principles have prominence in our core values, a great legacy becomes a sure thing.

※

This might seem like an odd way to close a book on culture. But this is the key to the difference between great culture and a bad culture. Our instruction book is the Bible, and all these character principles we've discussed are found in it. When we follow these teachings, they will become our core values; and when that happens, we will create great cultures wherever we go. That is what all believers are called to do: to be the lighthouse in a dark and tumultuous world.

The hatred alive and well in our day is not of God but of the evil one. However, in true fashion, the ungodly accuse Christ followers of being haters when we push back against sinful practices. People assume the deep division in our country is political. It is not. In John 15:19, Jesus clearly states why we are hated by many: "If you were of the world, the world would love you as its own; but because you are not of this world, but I chose you out of the world, therefore the world hates you" (ESV).

This is why the God-honoring life is like swimming upstream. The forces of darkness are like a strong current, and it's easy to just float along if we become one of them. If no one pushes back on our beliefs, we aren't being bold and productive. If keeping our mouths shut and not proclaiming the truth was the right thing to do, then why did they take Jesus and torture and execute Him in the heinous fashion that they did? They thought by killing Him they would forever stamp out His works and all of Christianity. And how did that work out?

On Good Friday, we remember the death of Jesus, which would change the world forever. His work on earth was done, and the last words He uttered on the cross were "It is finished." No longer did His followers need to kill and sacrifice animals to pay for their sins. The Son of God was willing to die for us so that our salvation could be free, and millions of people have chosen and are choosing to believe and accept His teachings. On Easter morning, He was resurrected from death to life to fulfill His prophecy. And that's what gives us the hope and faith that no other religion can give. He is alive and is going to return, and we will see Him face-to-face.

There is only one type of legacy that will last throughout the ages, and that is the legacy of God-fearing men and women. If our accomplishments have been to work hard, raise a family in a great God-fearing culture, and help to further the Kingdom by our giving, then we will have accomplished much and our rewards will be great. If we are looking for fame and fortune, we will be sadly disappointed.

Jesus spoke about rewards in Matthew 5:

> "God blesses those who are poor and realize their need for him,
> for the Kingdom of heaven is theirs.
> God blesses those who mourn, for they will be comforted.
> God blesses those who are humble, for they will inherit the whole earth.
> God blesses those who hunger and thirst for justice,
> for they will be satisfied.
> God blesses those who are merciful, for they will be shown mercy.
> God blesses those whose hearts are pure, for they will see God.
> God blesses those who work for peace,
> for they will be called the children of God.
> God blesses those who are persecuted for doing right,
> for the Kingdom of Heaven is theirs.
> God blesses you when people mock you and persecute you and lie about you and say all sorts of evil things against you because you are my followers. Be happy about it! Be very glad! For a great reward awaits you in heaven. And remember, the ancient prophets were persecuted in the same way."

Nothing could be further from the world's view of rewards, typified by *Time* magazine's man of the year, a Hollywood star with your name on it, being listed with Fortune 500 companies, or your picture on a calendar with all our previous presidents.

ഌ♦ഌ

Many are the obscure men and women who leave the greatest legacies. Billy Graham was spot on when he said, "The greatest legacy one can pass on to one's children and grandchildren is not money or other material things accumulated in one's life, but rather a legacy of character and faith." **Our legacies are grounded in our character and our faith.** These might only be two words, but both say volumes about who we really are. The Bible is our encyclopedia for both. It teaches us how to live and builds the foundation on which all our core values stand.

One of the golden keys to leaving this world a better place is doing our best in our gifted areas. A farmer who provides food for the world. A pastor who cares for a flock. A mother who nourishes and a nurse who cares. A carpenter, a plumber, an electrician, a mail carrier, a factory worker. Whatever it is that you do, give it all you've got, and when you breathe your last breath, you can say "I gave it my all and left this world a little better than when I was born into it."

Many years ago, I ran across this story illustrating a cowboy's take on serving others:

A cowboy was traveling to a cattle roundup on a seldom-used trail in a remote section of desert. Being powerfully thirsty and out of water, he sat on a stump to give himself and his buckskin horse a bit of rest. Looking into the distance, he saw what looked like a water pump but thought it was probably a mirage and only his imagination.

Upon further inspection, he found the pump. A baking powder can attached to the pump handle contained a sheet of brown wrapping paper on which a message had been written in pencil. The message read:

> This pump is all right as of June 1932. I put a new sucker washer into it and it ought to last five years. But the washer dries out and the pump has got to be primed. Under the white rock I buried a bottle of water, out of the sun and the cork end up. There's enough water in it to prime this pump, but not if you drink some water first. Pour in about ¼ of the

> water, let her soak to wet the leather. Then pour in the rest medium fast, and begin to pump. You'll get water. The well has never run dry. Have faith. When you get watered up, fill the bottle, and put it back like you found it for the next feller.
>
> Signed, Desert Pete
>
> P.S. Don't go drinking the water first! Prime the pump with it and you'll git all you can hold. And next time you pray, remember that God is like the pump. He has to be primed. I've given my last dime away a dozen times to prime the pump of my prayers, and I've fed my last beans to a stranger while saying Amen. It never failed yet to git me an answer. You got to git your heart fixed to give before you can be given to.

Desert Pete's story has been told with varying details in various media, one of which is a song written by Billy Edd Wheeler and recorded by the Kingston Trio. Google it. It's a catchy old song, and even if bluegrass might not be your cup of tea, it will still inspire you. Ponder the deeper meaning of leaving some water for the next person who comes along.

※

So to leave the world a better place and leave a culture with our name on it, we all need to be intentional about building our legacy. There are many ways to do this. Helping our fellow man is high on the list.

A set of goals I make for myself each year has been my guide for strengthening the culture at our workplace and in our home. Every January 1, I review the past year's goals to see if there are any carryovers that deserved to be added to the new year's list.

Five of these appear on my list every year. These I can jot down by memory. Those I've forgotten probably aren't worth mentioning. Here are the five that appear every year:

1. **Start each day** by having my coffee in my favorite chair in my office overlooking our farm; watching the sunrise while spending time in reading my Bible and devotional; and praying for the events of the day or whatever is coming up on my calendar. Instead of running off after breakfast and diving into the schedule for the day, observing this little habit has done me much good. If I miss a morning due to an early morning meeting, I feel unprepared for the day. Many devotionals are available, and one of my favorites is written by my friend Steve Wingfield. *Guiding Principles to Live, Learn, and Lead* contains all 48 of our Lodestar principles and is a great way to start every day. Many a day holds challenges and conversations that are critical and may be difficult. To face the day after first having a chat with God will give us great confidence and wisdom.

2. **Treat each person with dignity and respect.** This is operating by the Golden Rule Jesus gave us in Matthew 7:12: "Do to others whatever you would like them to do to you. This is the essence of all that is taught in the law and the prophets." Powerful words. The Golden Rule is truly golden. The first person that word "others" applies to is the spouse we live with. Treat your spouse with great respect and love. Every day, Gladys and I tell each other we love each other, and we do not retire for the night with something that has come between us that day still unresolved. To let the issue simmer and grow will lead to resentment. Much can be learned about a person by watching how they treat their spouse. If they denigrate each other, they will do the same to you. Bottom line: Don't trust a person who speaks harshly to their spouse.

In the workplace and in all walks of life, the Golden Rule has become a nearly unrecognized principle in our world today. But it is at the very core of any great culture. Without observing this principle, it is virtually impossible to achieve long-lasting success.

This verse is often taken out of context and used in the wrong way. In our workplace, we held people accountable for their actions, and when we've had to let people go, a common reaction was that we weren't following the Golden Rule. But holding people accountable is not only essential for all of us, it's biblical. As the leader of our company for 40 years, I was a stickler for this principle of accountability. Another one of the things we stressed was that our purchasing people would treat our suppliers with respect and kindness. Without good vendors we don't exist. However, holding them accountable was also a must. No relationship can survive for long periods of time without these two principles, Respect and Accountability.

One of my strengths is that I do not mince words and I say it like it is. I want to be respectful always, but to dance around a conversation that is confrontational is not my style. Following up afterward with words of affirmation and kindness is the key. The hard conversation is unavoidable in a successful business, but to shun the other person and put them on your blacklist is wrong.

3. **Forgiveness.** In my 70 years, I have done many things for which I needed to ask forgiveness. It is not a sign of weakness but of strength and character. Asking God to forgive us of our wrongdoings and sins is easy, but if our actions or words have harmed another person, we need to ask their forgiveness. The Holy Spirit will prompt us to do this, and if we don't obey that prompt, relationships can remain broken for a lifetime. If the other person fails to forgive us after we asked for forgiveness, the burden of unforgiveness will be placed on their shoulders

and we are free and clear. Just lately I went back to an old friend of more than 40 years and asked for forgiveness for inappropriate actions and we were reconciled. The person might have forgotten about what I'd done, but I hadn't and it weighed heavily on my conscience. It feels great to be free and clear of that weight on my shoulders.

When you are the one who is wronged, not everyone will ask for your forgiveness. Forgive the offender anyway. It doesn't mean you will have a close relationship with the other person, but the fifty-pound weight is no longer in your backpack. Yes, the unforgiving person is also carrying a heavy burden. Again, I recommend you get a copy of the most profound book I have ever read on this subject, Paul J. Meyer's *Forgiveness: The Ultimate Miracle.* The book is an eye-opening account of how this principle affects who we are and how we live our lives. Meyer's stories show us the power of forgiveness as well as the destructive power of unforgiveness. Those two incredibly strong forces can change your life. That's why the Lord's Prayer includes, "Forgive us our debts as we forgive our debtors."

4. **Love people for who they are** and not for who you wish they were. The Bible has much to say about love. "Three things will last forever—faith, hope, and love—and the greatest of these is love" (1 Corinthians 13:13). It is specific in our love for others, but has strong words for those whose love is simply turned inward.

> You should know this, Timothy, that in the last days there will be very difficult times. For people will love only themselves and their money. They will be boastful and proud, scoffing at God, disobedient to their parents, and ungrateful. They will consider nothing sacred. They will be unloving and unforgiving; they will slander others and have no self-

> control. They will be cruel and hate what is good. They will betray their friends, be reckless, be puffed up with pride, and love pleasure rather than God. They will act religious, but they will reject the power that could make them godly. Stay away from people like that! (2 Timothy 3:1-5)

This describes the days we are living in to a T, on the world stage and in our country. Note that this passage says these things will be prevalent "in the last days."

5. **Be generous** with those who have chosen to spend the best years of their lives with our company and work under my leadership. Any success we have experienced was produced by the best group of people I have ever met. If you were to ask them why they chose Weaver Leather as their choice of a career, few would say they did so because of their deep love for leather or the products we made from leather. Few would say their choice was made because of the money they could earn. Some might say the animal markets we serve, such as equine, livestock, and pet brought them to work for us. But the vast majority would tell you they chose our company because of its culture. Some employees came to us from bad culture companies and have never left our company. We have many long-term team members, those with 10, 20, 30, 40 and more years of service. When your people are connected to more than a paycheck, the results are amazing.

The question I asked myself many times was that if our compensation package was equal or better than any other company around and someone was looking for a job that matched their skills, would they choose us? Now before I answer that, I can assure you that we have some great companies to choose from in our area. None are perfect, but many have great cultures. But I believe people will ultimately pick companies that have leaders who are people of faith, people of character, and people who have a generous mindset.

This generosity goes beyond what's going to be in an employee's paycheck. It also determines what the owner does with the earnings of the company. Generosity is contagious. We have had a benevolence fund at our workplace for years, and we all chip in and help those in our corporate family who might have fallen on hard times, have lost a spouse or child, or had medical bills that went over and above what insurance would cover. We have had other initiatives such as supplying water wells and clean drinking water in countries that lacked water purification. We held a fundraiser for this mission at the end of the year and were astounded what was raised. The company matched every dollar that our people contributed. I later found out that some of our people gave their Christmas bonuses to this cause. Yes, all of it. Generosity is a heart condition. It's not done by compulsion or coercion; it's done by people with grateful hearts who want to share with those less fortunate. This principle of a great culture might be the strongest bond that holds people together. When the company wins, we all win.

And generosity goes even further than the boundaries of our company. The promise I made to Almighty God on that cold morning in November on the day of my dad's funeral was that if He helped me, I would give back to Him through worthy causes a minimum of 10 percent of every dollar we ever made for as long as I owned the company. It was this blessing, investment, or whatever you want to call it, that took us from a handful of people to between 300 to 400 employees and our customer base from a few dozen to many thousands. (That prayer is also a big reason we have so many outstanding employees. My second request that day was that God would bring us the right people at the right time. He did this in ways that still amaze me.)

Generosity pays back enormous dividends. When we buy stocks, the company we've invested in may do very well over a period of time, but at some point when new owners take control or new people come into leadership, we can see the stock start to decline. At times we even see it falling so far that we're losing money. But what we give away can never be diminished, and it will last forever.

Living a life of generosity can be summed up with the famous quote by Zig Ziglar: "You can have everything in life you want, if you will just help other people get what they want." It goes against our human nature to give to others, especially if we see them doing foolish things with what they have. In this country, there are very few people who have worked hard, given it their all, asked others for good advice, and made good choices, who then became destitute. But none of those factors are the criteria for our giving. Our mandate is to give to the poor, and to withhold help when these criteria aren't met would leave many in dire circumstances. To help people put food on the table and a roof over their heads is our responsibility as believers. Period. When we do that with the organizers and churches in the area and they present the Gospel along with the aid, we truly are the hands and feet of Jesus. That is our calling and our ultimate goal: to help as many suffering people as we can and to bring the Gospel to them. That's what the Great Commission is all about.

The giving principle is one of the mainstays of the great-culture person, family, church, and business. When we teach, mentor, and help someone along life's journey, we set an example for others, and that's how culture is built, one person at a time.

I hope that this book is an encouragement to every man and woman who reads it. We will never know who was watching us and was influenced to follow the pathway of achieving great character, great faith, and leaving this world a better place in the days they were given.

ꕥ♦ꕥ

My mom and dad were by no means perfect. Dad was inconsistent in his parenting. The fact that they had a bad marriage didn't help the situation, but his harsh punishments and strict rules to live by created a bad culture in our home. I have forgiven my parents, but the scars remain. They are healed over scars, but they have affected my adult life. I now look back and realize that I also was far from the perfect father to my kids. My siblings have also suffered effects from our dysfunctional childhood home.

To most people, Mom and Dad were the average parents who worked hard, never had more than they needed, and lived a simple life without any frills. So what, if anything, was their legacy?

Dad taught me about absolute integrity and honesty. To my knowledge, he never defrauded anyone. He paid his bills on time, every time. He gave to those in need and supported the church he and Mom attended. His word was his bond, and the mention of his name gained us a high credit rating with our vendors. He was bold and courageous and spoke the truth to people who probably didn't want to hear it. He left us with a fledgling company that has blessed its employees, customers, suppliers, and the industries we serve.

A timid and shy person, Mom did not want to be in the limelight. She was a diehard introvert, a trait which she so generously passed on to me. Mom, a wonderful cook and baker, gave me orderliness, the desire to have things neat and clean. Weaver Leather reflects that to this day. She was humble and never strived to be noticed, and she loved me. I was her favorite until my brother came along 12 years later, and then he became her pride and joy.

The legacy my parents gave me helped to shape my life in terms of faith and values. And that small startup company has become the source for our giving to help people in many parts of the world. They just didn't live to see their hard work turn into a huge blessing. I am quite certain they are enjoying their delayed rewards in Heaven today.

Great culture is contagious, and if everyone influences only 10 people in their lifetime, we'll make a big difference. If there are one hundred million faithful Christ followers in our country, we would touch and influence one billion people. Think about that.

The goal for all of us is to finish well and to hear the words, "Well done, my good and faithful servant" (Matthew 25:23). May we all remain faithful, no matter what the future brings.

APPENDIX

The Lodestar Guidance Principles

Components of a Great Culture

The Lodestar Principles

I believe one of the ways we can leave a legacy that makes the world a better place is by living and teaching good character. This is a brief overview of The Lodestar Guidance program we put into place in our company. My friend Steve Wingfield reminds us that "If we do not take the opportunity to equip future generations with the tools required to live and lead successfully, they are destined to repeat the failures that plague our nation today."

As you read about each of the 48 Lodestar character principles, ask yourself this question: What might happen if our company, workplace, home, or small group would study these 48 principles in depth and learn how they can first change us and then also become guiding principles in the culture of our home and business?

Each principle comes with a bulletin explaining the character trait in detail, a study guide, and a video depicting the principle in real-life situations. At our company, we have an all-company meeting once a month, watch the video, and then talk about the principle and how it can be used in our workplace. We give character recognition awards to first-year employees and to those who are nominated as shining stars of that day's principle. The remainder of the 30- to 40-minute meeting is dedicated to letting everyone know how the company is doing in terms of sales and profit goals, and also to announce what's coming up that everyone should be aware of. We close the meeting with a prayer. In the past, we would also have smaller groups of 10 meet and participate in more in-depth sessions of studying and discussing the bulletins. The response from our people has been overwhelmingly positive.

We have done this for over 20 years, and the result is a culture that is shaped by these principles. It's a great way for the company's leader to share and teach what they hold dear. And when we teach this character program, we soon figure out that we need to live out what we teach. It holds us accountable, and well it should.

This is one way we can leave a lasting legacy and set people up for success in life, leadership, and the home. To learn more about Lodestar Guidance and how to subscribe, you can go to lodestarguidance.com and watch a demo video, and contact the Lodestar office at (540) 236-5982 or (800) 729-2239, and ask for Luke Weaver. Lodestar Guidance is at 4153 Quarles Court, Harrisonburg, VA 22801.

The Lodestar Principles

These 48 qualities taught by the Lodestar program can shape our future and influence our children and young people to become men and women of character, faith, and leadership.

1. Forgiveness

Life is a rough and tumble place. No matter how hard we try, we will offend people and people will offend and hurt us. To forgive and ask forgiveness shows incredible strength, not weakness. Unforgiveness will hinder us more than we can imagine. Even if the situation wasn't entirely our fault, we can still ask forgiveness for offending another. The most healing words we can speak are "I'm sorry. Can you forgive me?"

2. Compassion

A prevalent attitude is to judge those who have fallen on hard times and say, "If it were not for their stupid decisions, they wouldn't be in the place they are." But we are to help the needy no matter what their past looks like. That's true compassion, and true compassion is a principle worthy of reward. We receive part of the immediate rewards in our own bodies and souls. Compassionate acts lower the level of cortisol, the hormone produced in our bodies by stress, by as much as 23 percent, and increase DHEA, a hormone that counteracts the aging process, by 100 percent. Compassionate people also have a much higher degree of self-satisfaction and inner peace.

3. Courage

Courage is so important that the Greek philosopher Aristotle believed "Courage is the first of human virtues because it makes all others possible." This is a virtue everyone wants and needs, but there's a price to pay. The price is that when we try something, it may tank and make us look foolish. Courage knows the chance of failure is very real. But fear is an emotion that should never guide our steps; emotions are fickle, and fear can keep us from moving forward only because we're tired and unsure of ourselves. After careful consideration, courage makes a decision to move ahead and cast all doubt aside. And many times, even a failure on the first try leads to answers for the second try.

4. Accountability

When we give people permission to speak into our lives if they see we're venturing into forbidden or dangerous territory, we are setting up checkpoints that will steer us away from hardships and trouble. Powerful politicians, business leaders, and pastors as well as ordinary husbands, wives, and friends all have temptations that will ultimately hurt or destroy those who are too proud to hear from a designated friend that trouble is ahead. Staying accountable can save us from much pain down the road. The issue can be as simple as showing up late for your job, or it can be as serious as cheating on your spouse. Without accountability, we walk on a high wire of risk. Ask a well-respected friend to hold you accountable. It's the safest way to do life.

5. Patience

Waiting in line at a restaurant, an amusement park, or in traffic causes me to feel trapped, and I look for an alternative. On a scale of 1 to 5, my patience is about a 2.5. I'm not alone in the "impatient" category; most people are impatient. Our society has most things available at the click of a key on computer or phone. Amazon is the friend of all impatient people. But impatient people tend to be impulsive, and impulsive people tend to make poor decisions. Impatient people also tend to have relationship problems. My impatience makes this principle one of my least favorite to talk about, but it is one of the virtues we are asked to have as believers. Patient people will let a scenario unfold before jumping into decisions. Patient people pray for something and then wait on the Lord's leading. It's a fallacy that patience is simply ceasing all forward movement and twiddling your thumbs while you wait. Patient people wait actively, doing what they can while waiting. Listen to a good podcast while waiting in traffic. Take the time to learn and grow. The good news is that while I'm still only at 2.5 on this scale, I once was a 1.

6. Diligence

Ever see someone who is a strong starter but a poor finisher? Remember this: Starters are many, but finishers are few. The end goal is exciting, but at the first roadblock, those who get distracted, procrastinate, and neglect what needs to be done to keep the drive alive, will be sidelined. When the goal is indelibly etched in our minds and all systems are go, the end goal becomes a priority. We might get sidetracked for a day or two, but the focus must shift back to the project at hand. Face it, a person who has many projects in his area of responsibility will neglect some of them. So if you want to do everything yourself and not delegate, then don't go down any more rabbit trails until you finish what you started. Diligence is laser-like focus to steadfastly finish the race. There are no rewards for those who don't finish.

7. Initiative

One of the first signs of leadership I see in a person is that they do what needs to be done without being asked to do it. Some people simply don't see a problem or the next step in a project. Others see it but are fearful of doing something because the "something" might not be done right. Another group of people may see the next step clearly, but procrastinate. And then there are those who have a union mentality and say "It's not my job." These attitudes all disqualify one for leadership positions, and that's why dynamic leaders are rare birds and they usually get snatched up quickly by the best companies at the best pay levels. Initiative and leadership are normally found in the same person, and those chosen few will be rewarded for a job well done.

8. Attitude

Zig Ziglar has said, "It's your attitude, not your aptitude that will determine your altitude." We have no control over many things in life, but we do control our attitude. Positive attitudes and negative attitudes are both chosen by the individual. Attitude is a by-product of the way we think and what we choose to dwell on. When it comes to leadership, people with a great attitude are magnets that attract good people. The opposite is also true; people with negative and bad attitudes repel people. Choose a good attitude. It will put you at an altitude that's less bumpy.

9. Influence

When we have no influence, people will only follow our lead if they are coerced. That is true both in the workplace and in the home. Influence could be the most important principle of the 48, but it can be zapped by three things: 1) When our main focus is on ourselves. 2) When we are rude and unkind. 3) If we lack integrity in our morals, our work, and our promises. The sobering fact is we are all under close scrutiny by our families, our co-workers, and most of all by the God we serve. When we breech someone's trust, our influence goes out the door. Without the character shaped by the other 47 principles, we will have no influence. Influence is like gold in our relationships; it is rare and it is precious. It can be squandered by just one act of poor character. And when that happens, our only way to restore it is to humble ourselves and ask forgiveness from those we have hurt and from God.

10. Productivity

"Make it your ambition to lead a quiet life: You should mind your own business and work with your hands, just as we told you, so that your daily life may win the respect of outsiders and so that you will not be dependent on anybody." This self-help advice is found in the Bible in 1 Thessalonians 4:11-12 (NIV). God made us capable of producing incredible results. He never meant us to live off other people's money, as in government assistance. In such cases, the church should be providing help to those who need it. The Amish are the best example of this principle I have seen. They do not accept money from the government; they take care of their own; they work with their hands and live quiet lives; they raise much of their own food; they work hard and don't know the meaning of "retirement"; they help each other in any way they can; and even in cases of those who are handicapped, they find ways to be productive. One of the factors leading to the downfall of our country is the idleness that leads to many destructive habits. Who can feel good about themselves if they are not working and productive? Work is not a punishment; it is a gift that our Creator gave us to use. Use the gift wisely and reap its rewards.

11 Empathy

Alfred Adler defined empathy as "seeing with the eyes of another, listening with the ears of another, and feeling with the heart of another." Seeking first to understand and then to be understood is a powerful tool. You will find a heart more receptive to your message if the other person feels that their viewpoint has been understood. The Bible tells us, "Be happy with those who are happy, and weep with those who weep" (Romans 12:15). Many times, I have changed my mind about other people's actions after I learned about their circumstances. Everyone will flinch when someone touches their sore spot; and everyone *does* have their sore spots. The only way to avoid these sensitivities is to know what they are before communicating. Empathy is not about tiptoeing around others, but it's learning about others' hurts and hang-ups *and* their joys and celebrations.

12 Restraint

When I took a class to get my concealed carry permit, we spent as much time talking about how to defuse a situation as we did learning how to effectively defend ourselves. We learned that the use of deadly force should be a last resort and not a first. That takes restraint. In life, restraint is often a little pause that will change our answer or actions. Philip Massinger said "He that would govern others, first should be the master of himself." Our world is sadly in need of this principle today. People attack on social media and hide behind their computers; many seem to have lots of unresolved anger, ready to explode at any time; road rage is a loss of control over one's actions. We are most vulnerable to a loss of restraint when we are tired or are carrying simmering anger from unresolved issues. It's easier to show restraint if we recognize this in ourselves and realize now is not the time to respond to something or try to fix a problem. When you feel like lashing out, hit the pause button. Think. Listen. And maybe get a good night's sleep before you respond.

13 Sincerity

Dad did. Now I do too. We say it like it is, with all sincerity. We don't sugarcoat it. People-pleasing was not one of Dad's traits, and it's not one of mine. Jesus said, "Do to others as you would have them do to you." I want others to tell me the unembellished truth, and I respect them when they do. I want to understand exactly what the person is trying to convey to me, and if the message is negative but true, I will thank them. It's difficult to grow as a person if no one has the courage and sincerity to speak into your or my life, even when the truth is something that could offend us. Sincerity is telling a vendor the real reason you don't buy from them anymore. How can someone correct a mistake if they don't know the truth? Romans 12:9 packs so much into a few words. The verse begins with "Love must be sincere," so it is an act of love to be sincere and totally honest with one another.

I know that sincerity can get you into trouble these days; people are quickly labeled "haters" and accused of "hate speech." But the second part of Romans 12:9 tells us that Christ followers are called to hate what is evil and cling to what is good. Dare to speak the truth, and do it in sincere love.

14 Development

Zig Ziglar said it best and repeated this many, many times. "You were born to win, but to be a winner, you must plan to win, prepare to win, and expect to win."We were born to win, but just that in itself is no guarantee. Winning depends on how serious we are about planning and preparing to win. Nobody ever won a gold medal, got into the Hall of Fame, or succeeded in anything without intense and intentional development. Our gifts and talents are of no value unless we work hard at learning, growing, and persevering. The journey is all about developing ourselves to be ready for the time we can compete. My friend Steve always says, "You gotta have the want to." Nobody can take the "want to" away from you, no matter if you grew up in a bad home or made some bad choices in your life. If you have a burning desire to succeed and you put the time and effort into what you want to do and to be, you are on the right track. Get all the information you can gather from books and from people who have gone before you, and in due time, you will win. Just make sure your goal is worthy of your efforts and the sacrifices you will need to make along the way.

15 Discernment

It's easy to say *yes* or *no* to 80 percent of the choices we must make. It's the remaining 20 percent of our decisions that we sometimes struggle with—and those are the decisions that bring

80 percent of our success. Discernment is given to us if we ask for it. God told King Solomon that he could ask for whatever he wanted and God would grant it. Of all the things Solomon could have requested, including long life or wealth, he asked for a discerning heart to govern his people and to distinguish right from wrong. The Lord was pleased with his request and made Solomon the wisest man that ever lived. We serve the same God Solomon did, and He still gives us discernment when we ask for it and diligently read His words in the Bible.

16 Fairness

My guess is that everyone has been hurt at some time by unfair treatment. Life itself is not fair. Fairness as a character trait is not about what we experience in our lifetime; fairness is about how we treat other people. You can tell a great deal about a person if you watch how they treat people who can't do anything for them. If they treat the president of the company very differently than the janitor, that's being unfair. We were born with an "unfair" nature. Kids on the playground treat others unfairly when their clothes don't come up to today's standards. Being fair to everyone is a choice, even when we have no idea who they are or what their life is like. Again, living out the Golden Rule also requires the fairness principle.

17 Kindness

Kindness is a first cousin to fairness. Kindness has a boomerang effect. Try saying "Good morning" to complete strangers. Usually, they will reciprocate, and if not, don't worry about it. Today's culture is not very friendly. Sit on a bench and watch people as they walk by. Not many smiles or even acknowledgment of other people's presence. Principle #9 was influence, and one of the fastest ways to gain influence is to be kind. Kindness is free, it makes you feel good, and it draws people to you. Mother Teresa nailed it when she said, "Let there be kindness in your face, in your smile, in the warmth of your greeting… Don't only give your care, but give them your heart as well." Try kindness for one day and see what a difference it makes, not just in others' reactions but in your own demeanor as well.

18 Loyalty

Just because my wife has habits that annoy me at times doesn't mean that I am not fiercely loyal to her. Loyalty means that I will be with you whether you are right or wrong. Loyalty also means that if you are wrong, I will tell you—instead of talking to others about you—and will help you make it right. I have always tried to be very loyal to the people who have chosen to work for me, but that also meant I talked to them when they messed up. Loyalty is caring enough to hold people accountable in a kind and supportive way. In politics, loyalty for the party you identify with does not mean you cover wrongdoing. In 1974, many Republicans voted yes to impeach Richard Nixon. Today, that would not happen. The "loyalty" of politics today is not true loyalty. It's misguided loyalty.

19 Orderliness

You might think this is a rather odd character principle to include—but have you ever worked with a disorderly person? Or worked at a company that was disorderly? It's very frustrating. My mom ran a tight ship. Her house was spotless, and nothing about her was disorderly. That was my normal as a kid growing up, and guess what? The habits stayed with me as I got older. Our company has always kept things clean and orderly. Not only do our people enjoy working in a place that's clean and neat but our guests take notice as they tour our plant, warehouse, and offices. We had a banker who visited us years ago; I met with him after his tour, and his first comments were about how well-kept everything was and the cleanliness of the floors and work area. His said, "I knew in the first five minutes of my tour that your company was a first-class place. My theory is dirty floors, dirty books." I never forgot that. Ten minutes before quitting time, everyone on the plant floor cleans up their own area. The next morning, they start the day in a clean and orderly environment. It's a reflection on who we are as a company and on the character of our people.

20 Motivation

"Just waiting for my next ship to come in." That was the favorite reply from one of my friends whenever we ran into each other and I asked him how he was doing. It was humorous, but for many people, it's a true depiction of their lives. They are waiting for good things to start happening to them, making no forward movement on their own initiative. Many times, this is a result of having too many things on one's plate; then, the only things that get done are those that need the most attention at that moment. Like almost all of these principles, motivation is a choice, not an emotion. If we are in a leadership role of any kind, we are the pace car. We can never expect our people to move at a faster pace than we are running. The bottom line: Motivated people motivate people. Over the years, I have mentored and taught many team leaders, and even though everyone has faults and shortcomings, a lack of motivation *cannot* be one of them if they want to lead a team. So establish long-term goals, break them down to little short-term goals, and keep hitting those goals day by day.

21 Boldness

Time magazine ran an article that stated, "Bold people are rated highest for such qualities as general intelligence, dependability, and self-discipline." The first person who comes to mind on the principle of boldness is Elon Musk. The man appears to be fearless when it comes to reaching his objectives. He sees a need and fills it; he is not afraid to speak his mind and criticism doesn't faze him. He is also the wealthiest man on the planet (as of this writing). Today's society doesn't have many Elon Musks. When someone criticizes us, we're much more likely to shut down and shut up. The extreme far left people in our world are vastly outnumbered but their voices are heard and feared by most. It's because they are bold, brash, and unafraid—and look how far they have come in their deranged causes. We, the majority, are busy minding our own business and don't pay any attention to them until their agenda affects us and our children. At that point, it's a little late to become vocal. On this principle, I rank high; I've never been accused of being timid. We have no reason to be timid and fearful because 2 Timothy 1:7 tells us "For God has not given us a spirit of fear and timidity, but of power, love, and self-discipline." Our best efforts plus an almighty God will *always* make us a majority.

22 Wisdom

Every one of us is born with a certain level of intelligence and certain gifts and talents, but no one comes into this world with wisdom. King Solomon said this: "Fear of the LORD is the foundation of wisdom. Knowledge of the Holy One results in good judgment" (Proverbs 9:10). All the knowledge and teaching of man comes from mankind, created by God. Only the Creator Himself knows our thoughts and gave us the ability to learn. He knows our hearts; He knows our future and our past. He knows the answer before we even know the question. And that's why He says, "Trust in the LORD with all your heart and lean not on your own understanding. In all your ways submit to Him, and he will make your paths straight" (Proverbs 3:5-6 NIV). True wisdom comes from God and God alone. Ask for wisdom daily and read the Master's words because He is the single source for true wisdom.

23 Ownership

The ownership we're talking about is not owning "stuff," it's assuming responsibility for our outcomes and results. Leadership in its purest form is owning what we set into motion. It doesn't matter if we own the company or not. If we are given a job or task to accomplish, it's up to us to complete it and see it through to fruition. Many have a tendency to own something until problems arise—and then they'll play the blame game when success is not achieved. We are not only accountable for what we do; we are just as accountable for the things we did not do. The easiest way to have someone fully understand a goal or an objective and to take ownership is to explain why it's important. When I was a little boy, I would question why Dad wanted me to do certain tasks. If he wasn't in a good frame of mind, he would say, "Because I said so." Ever say that to anyone? I am quite sure I have, but it doesn't inspire the other person to take ownership of the task at hand. Explaining the importance and the why can change one's motivation to do the job with diligence.

24 Likeability

Guy Kawasaki, marketing specialist and author, says "The three pillars of a personal brand are trustworthiness, likeability, and competence." The chances of one's success are largely based on how people see us. Likeability is a magnet that draws people to us and makes them willing to help us. Being likeable is a way of life, not just occasional moments of amicability. Characteristics of likeable people are: humor, encouraging words, listening, helpfulness, and gratitude. They have a good sense of humor and are enjoyable to be with. They are "lifters," not "drainers," and we feel energized when we come away from being with them. The cost of leadership without likeability is very high. We'll lose people, no matter how much we pay them. Our customers and vendors will leave us if something better comes along. When the center of our attention is ourselves and what's good for us, people lose interest. *The Like Ability Factor* by Tim Sanders is a great read and sheds some very important light on this subject.

25 Integrity

Integrity is much more than being honest in business dealings and not cheating people. Integrity is being who we say we are. Over the years, some of the people with whom I had the best interviews turned out to be the worst hires. They said one thing, but lived another. To live with integrity encompasses so many of our other principles, like accountability and transparency, loyalty and dependability, sincerity and fairness. Integrity also requires self-awareness. The person we tend to lie to the most is ourself. We need to know who we are and then be who we are. And if we aren't where we want to be on some of these principles, then teachability, determination, and self-control must also come into play.

26 Passion

Anyone who knows me knows that I score very high in this principle; I am either all in or all out. Life is too short to continuously do things for which we have no passion. In my younger years, I was passionate about the game of golf. I loved the challenge and the fellowship with my friends, but after my back surgeries, I was unable to play the game without triggering lots of pain. A friend took me to a sporting clay course, and I developed an even greater passion for this sport. The result was that two of my good friends and I built a course. (If you're ever in the area, google Airport Ridge Sporting Clays and you will see just how passionate I am about this.) As I get older, my passions and goals have changed. My greatest passions now are to 1) Serve my Lord and Savior Jesus Christ and to help others find Him and enjoy a God-centered life. 2) To help those in need, to fight poverty, to find ministries that help the helpless, and in so doing introduce them to the God that changes lives. 3) To help people who have businesses and share my experience with them. As we get older, our focus should shift from "me" to "them." Jesus gave us the command to help others, and the rewards we long for are tied to this concept. Passion gives us influence and influence brings opportunity to help others. Passionate people attract passionate people. And when there are two or more passionate, God-fearing people—Katie, bar the door! Something big is about to happen!

27 Self-awareness

My guess is that if we asked six people who know us well to describe who they think we really are, their answers would probably surprise us. And if they didn't have to sign their names on the questionnaire, it would really surprise us. The biggest obstacle in our lives is often our ego. The bigger the ego, the less effective a person is. We can call ego "being opinionated" or "competent" or anything else that's sugarcoated, but people who are an authority on almost everything are not fun to be around and not nearly as smart as they think they are. Paul wrote in Romans 12:3, "For by the grace given me I say to every one of you: Do not think of yourself more highly than you ought, but rather think of yourself with sober judgment, in accordance with the faith God has distributed to each of you" (NIV). Proverbs 26:12 warns, "Do you see a man who is wise in his own eyes? There is more hope for a fool than for him" (NIV). Being aware of our limitations is what makes us wise. The more accurate our view of our own character, motives, strengths, weaknesses, and how we relate to people, the more effective we will be.

28 Stewardship

I heard a pastor say that the best way to look inside a person's heart is to look at their checkbook. Jesus said, "For where your treasure is, there your heart will be also" (Matthew 6:21 NIV). As believers, we have been called to be both grateful for what we have been given and generous to causes that further the Kingdom. That, in a nutshell, is what this book is all about. As good stewards, we find ways to multiply our resources, not because we have an insatiable desire to have more for ourselves but because we are to work hard and be diligent to increase our resources for a larger purpose and plan. The farther we step out in faith and give sacrificially, the more God entrusts to us. That's where the greater rewards come into play. God connects the dots in our business efforts, we prosper, and then we help to supply the needs of those who are in desperate situations, thus garnering the rewards we are promised. The subject of stewardship is mentioned in the Bible hundreds of times, possibly more than almost any other subject.

29 Teachable

In order to be teachable, we need to know that we don't know it all. Those who believe they are an authority on almost everything won't be teachable; they're too proud. Those who are too busy will also not be teachable; they're too busy to look at new ideas and solutions. We can learn in many ways and become an authority on almost any topic if we read and research. Our minds are like sponges; whatever we pour in is ultimately who we become. When I started building our company, I read every good leadership book I could get my hands on. I listened to audio cassettes, went to seminars to hear the top leadership gurus, and talked to as many successful people as I could. Even so, I still made lots of mistakes. But for the teachable, even mistakes can be learning tools. John Maxwell said: "Sometimes you win, sometimes you learn." If we stay humble and realize that we have not reached the know-it-all stage (which will never happen), we will continue to learn and grow until we leave this world.

30 Transparency

Some people are open books, easily read. Some people are vaults, their lives lived in secrecy. The problem with the vault people is that they will never learn from others if they won't share their mistakes and deep, dark secrets with anyone. When we fail, we need to tell someone, especially when it affects other people. Asking for forgiveness is therapy for the heart. Proverbs 28:13 (NASB) says, "He who conceals his transgressions will not prosper, But he who confesses and forsakes them will find compassion." Transparency and admitting wrongs is not cowardly; it takes courage to become vulnerable and go against our human "sin" nature that would rather hide our wrongs. James 5:16 says, "Confess your sins to each other and pray for each other so that you may be healed." Another big advantage of being transparent is that we will be much better at communicating and connecting with people, and communication is a major part of leadership. Don't make people work to read between the lines; just say what you mean. And don't hide your true motives; that causes doubt and hinders trust.

31 Generosity

When we think of generosity, we usually think of giving or doing something for someone else when the recipient is the only one who benefits. Not true, research shows. Generosity is a foundational principle for mental health and relational health. It also reduces stress, supports physical health, enhances purpose, fights depression, and brings a host of other benefits that promote our psychological well-being. Generosity also makes us eligible to receive blessings and rewards that God sends our way. Even with all of these benefits and all that we have been given, the vast majority of people in this country give less than 4 percent of their income. Our president gave 3 percent of his annual income, and that's just what he reported. We are the wealthiest nation on the face of the earth, and we give less than half of what the Bible tells us to give, which is a minimum of 10 percent. Generosity is the best kept secret for success and fulfillment. Those who don't find this secret forfeit mental health benefits as well as rewards that last for eternity.

32 Humility

Humility is a misunderstood principle. It's not thinking less of ourselves or being a doormat for others to take advantage of. The humble person knows that no one is good at everything and simply accepts that. The proud person won't accept that fact and becomes a know-it-all. Humble people ask for good counsel and advice in order to make good decisions. Proud people do whatever seems right to them because they don't know what they don't know. I have a fast and steadfast rule: Don't do business with proud, arrogant people. Proud people are stubborn people. You can share all the facts you want and yet they will never change their minds because doing so would be admitting they were wrong. King Solomon said in Proverbs 11:14, "Where there is no guidance, a people falls, but in an abundance of counselors there is safety" (ESV). Pride is a deadly sin, and many a person has been bitten by its results.

33 Flexibility

A turn in the road can lead to a real disaster if we can't veer to the right or the left. Normally, our changes come in difficult times. That's why flexibility and faith should go hand in hand. We are uniquely made to live doing the perfect will of our Creator. If the Lord is the leader of our life and He has a mission for us, He will make it known by His nudging or a hardship that directs us into the channel in which He wants us. So the next time your life's journey takes you on a detour, ask Him what He has in mind and then listen and He will show you the way. Proverbs 19:21 says, "many are the plans in a person's heart, but it is the LORD's purpose that prevails" (NIV). So let's stay flexible and not go against His purpose.

34 Gratefulness

As we go through these 48 principles of character, you may have noticed that almost none of these come naturally for us. We were not born with good character. These are learned behaviors. Gratefulness is a good example of this. The abundance of things does not make one grateful, even if the "abundance" we're considering is our good health. Just this morning, I read the story of the ten lepers. Seeing Jesus as he was passing by, they called out, "Jesus, Master, have pity on us." In one little sentence, He told them to show themselves to the priests, and as they went, they were cleansed of this horrible and deadly disease. Only one came back and thanked Him. The nine others did not return to thank and honor the Lord for his miracle. I love this little quote by Joel Osteen: "Choosing to be positive and having a grateful attitude is going to determine how you're going to live your life." And that's living with an attitude of gratitude.

35 Resourcefulness

Every time you get in your car, use your phone, or flip on a light switch, you can thank someone for being resourceful. In the year 2020 alone, there were 388,900 patents granted by the U.S. Patent and Trademark office. Our country is blessed with many resourceful people who have made life much easier for all of us. In order to put this principle into effect, we need to embrace problems, limitations, and unforeseen circumstances as opportunities in disguise. Our Creator gave us minds capable of imagining what does not exist yet. Our job is to develop what we already have and always be on the lookout to improve something. My dad was quite resourceful, and watching how he would fix things with baler twine, wire, and duct tape made an impression on me as a youngster; and as I got older, I learned to be just as resourceful. That's how important it is to teach and model these character traits for our kids. It will make a difference in their lives.

36 Thoroughness

When you board a plane, do you glance into the cockpit and check out the pilot and copilot? I know I do, and I like to see some white hair on the pilots. It shows maturity, experience, and thoroughness as they go over their preflight checklist. Many lives are at stake, and one mistake could be fatal. That's why it's so important that there are two pilots on each flight. If one misses something or if something happens to one of them, the other pilot can fly and land the plane.

Over the years, I have made many decisions that could have affected our company negatively if we missed a key component of a process. Starting a project is a time when everyone is diligent and thorough, but as time goes by, the excitement wears off and things can get overlooked. To have a diverse team in charge gives me confidence in the process. There is an old saying that "the devil is in the details." And it's true. Starting strong but not sustaining thoroughness throughout the entire project can be a complete waste of the energy and cost of the project. To monitor and keep an eye on anything worth doing is wisdom in action.

37 Dependability

Neal A. Maxwell said it well in this quote: "God does not begin by asking us about our ability, but only about our availability. And if we then prove our dependability, he will increase our capability." I have seen this truth played out many times. Dependability might be one of the most desired traits we can hope for in a friend, partner, or coworker. People who have great ability but are not dependable give us a false sense of security because at some point they're likely to drop the ball. Jesus said this: "If you are faithful in little things, you will be faithful in large ones. But if you are dishonest in little things, you won't be honest with greater responsibilities" (Luke 16:10) {NLT} One of the biggest enemies of dependability is a schedule so full that we have no margin in life. The antidote for dangerous busyness is delegation. When I look at a resume for a coworker, partner, or team leader, I keep this little quote from Bob Jones in mind: "The greatest ability is dependability."

38 Self-Control

One of the hardest things in life is to control ourselves. Self-control is one of the attributes of the fruit of the Spirit listed in Galatians 5:22-23: love, joy, peace, patience, kindness, generosity, faithfulness, gentleness, and self-control. We weren't born with these attributes, but the good news is that when we invite Jesus into our hearts, the Holy Spirit is given residency there, and these are attributes He brings to our character. One needs only to watch the evening news to see the absence of the fruit of the Spirit. Yes, many people have grown up without having someone model these nine traits, but the real reason is the lack of godliness. The only way to have these qualities grow in our lives is to invite the Holy Spirit in and let Him work. He is the only cure for our lack of true self-control. Again, self-awareness and accountability are necessary. We will have little control over that which we are not aware of, and giving someone permission to speak into our lives is a good start to self-awareness and self-control.

39 Decisiveness

Show me someone who has never made a bad decision, and I will show you someone who hasn't made very many good decisions either. Worse than that, an indecisive person will never be successful, because they can't move ahead. One of the ways to make timely decisions is to set a deadline and then it's either *yes, no,* or *not now.* Making a decision is easier to do if we don't mind being wrong and making course corrections on the fly. But if we get too enamored with our decision and too proud to change, it becomes a poor decision. Doing nothing is by far the worst thing we can do. People in leadership have a responsibility to make timely decisions. If not, our team will lose confidence in our leadership ability. One of the first actions we as Christians should take when faced with a decision is to pray about it. God knows the outcome of every decision you're going to need to make. My prayer is always that He will open doors and show us it's a good move if it's a *yes* or that He will close doors if it's not a good move.

40 Honesty

Harvey Firestone, the founder of Firestone Tire and Rubber Co., said, "I believe fundamental honesty is the keystone of business." We are perhaps most tempted to be dishonest in the little things we say that aren't *quite* true or are only *half* true because we are reluctant to let the whole truth be known. Benjamin Franklin said, "Half a truth is often a great lie." Truth and honesty are not in high regard anymore, and it's one of the reasons our country is in a free fall. Politicians lie so smoothly, using half-truths about almost any subject that comes up, saying anything to gain power and control. This is certainly not true of all of them, but it's prevalent among the majority of our elected officials. Proverbs 12:22 says "The LORD detests lying lips, but he delights in people who are trustworthy" (NIV). It is noteworthy that Satan is the father of lies. He is cunning and knows how to use a truth, twist it, and change the meaning so that the lie actually seems to makes sense. The problem is there is no truth in him, and neither is there truth in those who choose him as their leader.

41 Punctuality

It might seem odd that punctuality is one of the 48 principles of our Lodestar Guidance program, but the lack of punctuality is not only annoying but is also disrespectful of other people's time. As an employer, I know how important punctuality is to relationships. This principle hits many buttons—and many people, regardless of position—in the way we do business. When we hire, we make an agreement to pay for work starting at 8:00 and quitting at 5:00 with specified breaks including lunch. When an employee breaches that agreement, the person needs to be held accountable, otherwise, it sends a bad message and becomes a problem. Every meeting we have should honor our commitment of time and the respect for the other person. When payment terms are 30 days, we should make sure our vendor has the payment in hand in 30 days. Being prompt on our commitments is the first sign that we are Christ followers. It will earn us many rewards from the people we deal with and from our all-seeing God.

42 Trustworthiness

Stephen Covey said it well with this little quote: "When the trust account is high, communication is easy, instant, and effective." Trustworthiness is a far-reaching character principle. It sends a strong message to your relationships that we will, without being told, censor how much we pass along to others. Our communication should be filtered by these four criteria: 1. Say what you mean and mean what you say. Don't promise what you can't deliver. 2. Put everything through a no-lie filter. A half-truth is not truth at all. If you are not sure, don't say it. 3. Live today as if it were your last day on Earth. 4. Let your *no* mean *no* and your *yes* mean *yes*. As difficult as #1 can be, learn to just say *no* when you are not able or do not want to do something. If your friend doesn't expect a no from you and is hurt when you do, your relationship probably isn't going to stand the test of time. Trust is a precious thing to have and earn. It can take a long time to build and an instant to destroy. The good news is that even though people will let us down at times, God *will* do what He said He would do. He's 100 percent trustworthy.

43 Determination

Know what is right, and never deviate from that. If we as believers would be as determined to do what is right and never give in to the wrong as our foes are determined to drive their agenda, we probably wouldn't be in the mess we're in today in this country. Remember, when the masses go a certain direction, it's usually the wrong way to go. Whether it's setting a business goal or desiring to stay on the path of honesty, integrity, and truth, don't give up just because others oppose or don't see your vision. Never give in, as Winston Churchill advised. However, don't confuse determination with just plain stubbornness. It's unwise to defend a position just because it's *your* idea. If a better idea comes along, embrace it and thank the person for it.

44 Discretion

To choose our words and actions carefully is important and not always easy to bite our tongue and consider the matter and the context it was said in. Sometimes it's better to say nothing if we are not certain on what to say—or not say. To choose our words and actions carefully is not always easy, but it's important to sometimes bite our tongue in consideration of the context and other factors. Sometimes no immediate answer is better than what we'd like to say in defense of our own thinking. Proverbs 19:11 says, "A man's discretion makes him slow to anger. And it is his glory to overlook a transgression" (NASB). The lack of discretion can lead to dangerous situations.

45 Innovation

Steve Jobs said "Innovation distinguishes between a leader and a follower." Today's term of "continued improvement" is pretty important. Business in general is a moving target, and what worked yesterday isn't necessarily going to work today. Technology is moving, and we either move with it or someone will eat our lunch. When the mentality is "If it isn't broke, don't fix it," forward movement is unlikely. This principle is as true in our personal lives as it is in business. Unless we are on a pathway that forces us to learn and grow, we will stagnate. Some people grow older and wiser, and some people just get older. Innovation is first seeing a need or opportunity and then using all our imagination and will power to meet that need or seize that opportunity. I call a spirit of innovation a healthy discontent. Which tent do you live in? Content or discontent? I choose a healthy discontent.

46 Joyfulness

Joy is another principle the Bible lists as a fruit of the Spirit. Happiness is an emotion that comes and goes; joy is a condition of the heart. I have noticed that grateful people are joyful people. It's easy to be joyful when we are grateful for the everyday things of life like a beautiful sunny day (in Ohio, that's something to be jubilant about). To slow down a bit and notice little things is medicine for the soul. My wife loves to feed and watch the birds. In the spring, the migrating birds return, and they're striking with their vivid colors. So when the first Baltimore oriole shows up, there is a celebration. That's gratitude, joyfulness, and happiness all rolled up in one. When the Bible tells us to guard our hearts, it means we're not to let anyone or anything rob us of our joy. Resentment and unforgiveness might be the biggest enemies of a joyful heart. We aren't in control of others' actions or wrongdoings; God says vengeance is His, and we need to let those emotions go. Perfectionism will also puncture joy—as long as we strive for perfection, we are not satisfied unless we achieve flawless result.

47 Focus

Roy Bennett wrote, "Focus on your strength, not your weakness. Focus on your character, not your reputation. Focus on your blessings not your misfortunes." *Focus.* Real focus is a powerful force, and the way we create a clear and intense focus is by setting clear, attainable goals. I've seen many starters but far fewer finishers. Focus is the rifle sighted in at 100 yards, and our focus places two or three shots in the 1" bullseye. A shotgun covers 24" at 40 yards, but it can't stop a charging bear. Many people use the shotgun approach and fail because their efforts, focus, and resources are diluted. To focus and take care of what you have will in return take care of you.

48 Respect

Respect is the glue that holds relationships together. Without respect, all is lost and we tend to go our separate ways. Fifty years ago, my wife and I said our wedding vows, and during the reception, one of the guests came over to our table and gave us a bit of advice. He said, "Paul, one of the secrets of a happy marriage comes from the principle of respect. No matter how frustrated you get with each other, never be disrespectful of one another, never say unkind or derogatory words, and never do things that belittle the other and go against the commitment you made just a few minutes ago." The fact that I remember this 50 years later is a testament to how his words impacted me. Our world today is sadly lacking respect. There are people I do not have respect for, but to be civil and polite is always the right thing to do. And the next time you see a veteran wearing a hat indicating his military service, stop and thank them for the sacrifice and service they gave our country. They will feel respected and you will feel the gratitude that came from this simple "Thank you for your service."

Milton Keynes UK
Ingram Content Group UK Ltd.
UKHW020705290124
436893UK00005B/32

9 781960 814029